Praise for *The 10 Key Ro* T000841

"I've never been one to wear hats. Some say it's because my head is too big, but that's another story. However, Dr. Gary McIntosh has helped me realize that to lead more effectively as a pastor I must wear various hats. In this book, hats represent the roles of a pastor, and I've never seen them defined so clearly. This book will help you lead better as soon as you engage it. We will be studying the book as a staff, and I encourage you to take a deep dive into the wisdom of my good friend Dr. McIntosh. Now that I think about it, I've never tried on a cowboy hat. I wonder if they have one in my size . . ."

Dr. Nelson Searcy, author and founding/teaching pastor, The Journey Church, New York City

"Pastors bearing a heavy load of demands and pressures have just been given a gift! This book simplifies the work of leading a church and is a practical tool for moving into an uncertain future."

Tom Harper, publisher, BiblicalLeadership.com; author of *Servant Leader Strong: Uniting Biblical Wisdom and High-Performance Leadership*

"Gary is known as a down-to-earth writer who provides principles that any pastor can use. He does not disappoint in this book. All pastors would agree with the ten key roles he identifies. The illustrations he shares come from his wealth of experience working with churches of all sizes. You will find the information about prioritizing your hats very helpful in implementing the insights provided."

Dr. Phil Stevenson, district superintendent, PSW Movement

Praise for *What Every Pastor Should Know*

"I love pastors. I am humbled by the fact that pastors often come to me for advice and wisdom. Now I have a resource that answers so many of their questions. This book is fantastic! There is no doubt that it will be on my shelf as a reference for years to come."

Thom S. Rainer, founder and CEO of Church Answers

"*What Every Pastor Should Know* is an invaluable reference book. Its value lies in being well researched, comprehensive, specific, and practical. It is also user friendly in listing so many guidelines and rules to help church leaders keep on course and not become sidetracked."

Eddie Gibbs, Donald A. McGavran Professor Emeritus of Church Growth at Fuller Seminary

"A wealth of insights for pastors on the day-to-day issues of leading an effective church."

Ed Stetzer, Billy Graham Distinguished Chair of Church, Mission, and Evangelism at Wheaton College

Praise for *Growing God's Church*

"Gary McIntosh is one of the leaders in research on growing churches. Anyone who is interested in knowing about growing churches should read this book. Everyone who is interested in actually working in a growing church needs to read this book."

Elmer L. Towns, cofounder and vice president, Liberty University

"A true gift to the kingdom. Every leader with a desire to fulfill the Great Commission should read *Growing God's Church* as soon as possible. The takeaways are revolutionary for the way we do outreach today."

Nelson Searcy, lead pastor of The Journey Church, New York City, founder of www.ChurchLeaderInsights.com, and author of *The Renegade Pastor*

the
solo
pastor

Understanding *and* Overcoming *the* Challenges
of Leading *a* Church Alone

GARY L. McINTOSH

BakerBooks

a division of Baker Publishing Group
Grand Rapids, Michigan

© 2023 by Gary L. McIntosh

Published by Baker Books
a division of Baker Publishing Group
PO Box 6287, Grand Rapids, MI 49516-6287
www.bakerbooks.com

Printed in the United States of America

All rights reserved. No part of this publication may be reproduced, stored in a retrieval system, or transmitted in any form or by any means—for example, electronic, photocopy, recording—without the prior written permission of the publisher. The only exception is brief quotations in printed reviews.

Library of Congress Cataloging-in-Publication Data
Names: McIntosh, Gary, 1947– author.
Title: The solo pastor : understanding and overcoming the challenges of leading a church alone / Gary L. McIntosh.
Description: Grand Rapids, MI : Baker Books, a division of Baker Publishing Group, [2023] | Includes bibliographical references.
Identifiers: LCCN 2022018516 | ISBN 9780801094897 (paperback) | ISBN 9781540903051 (casebound) | ISBN 9781493437702 (ebook)
Subjects: LCSH: Pastoral theology. | Loneliness—Religious aspects—Christianity. | Solitude.
Classification: LCC BV4013 .M39 2023 | DDC 253—dc23/eng/20220803
LC record available at https://lccn.loc.gov/2022018516

Unless otherwise indicated, Scripture quotations are from the (NASB®) New American Standard Bible®, Copyright © 1960, 1971, 1977, 1995 by The Lockman Foundation. Used by permission. All rights reserved. www.lockman.org

Scripture quotations labeled ESV are from The Holy Bible, English Standard Version® (ESV®), copyright © 2001 by Crossway, a publishing ministry of Good News Publishers. Used by permission. All rights reserved. ESV Text Edition: 2016

Scripture quotations labeled TLB are from The Living Bible, copyright © 1971. Used by permission of Tyndale House Publishers, Inc., Carol Stream, Illinois 60188. All rights reserved.

Baker Publishing Group publications use paper produced from sustainable forestry practices and post-consumer waste whenever possible.

23   24   25   26   27   28   29   7   6   5   4   3   2   1

To Dr. Glen S. Martin
September 3, 1953–July 8, 2021
A faithful pastor who inspired me;
a loving colleague who supported me;
a close friend who encouraged me.

Contents

Take Lessons First

If you want to fly an airplane, take lessons first.

—Anonymous

So, you want to learn to fly? Let me tell you a little secret that most pilots won't tell you. It's really easy to fly an airplane. It takes training, of course, but with about twenty hours of instruction, you'll know the basics and be ready to take off on your own. It takes many more hours and a lot more practice to master flying an airplane, but committing to a few steps will get you a private pilot's license. A few more hours and you'll have your instrument rating, and with even more hours you'll have a commercial pilot's license.

One of the steps in obtaining a private pilot's license is flying solo. After hours of reading manuals, listening to class lectures, and sitting alongside an instructor, the novice flyer must demonstrate their ability by flying the plane alone. It's called going solo or sometimes simply soloing. It means to do something alone, without an instructor.

The day a novice flyer solos is always an exciting one. While fledgling flyers are always a bit nervous, they anticipate being in the air controlling the plane alone. For most, soloing goes smoothly. They take off, fly their route, and return to the airport with little problem. For one of my friends, it was, well, more than exciting. His solo flight went just as planned until he tried to land at the airport. He touched down on the grass just short of the paved runway. Unfortunately, the grass was soggy from a recent rain and the tires dug deeply into the turf, causing the plane to flip over on its top. He found himself hanging upside down, supported only by his seat belt harness. Airport firefighters came to his rescue, and he was helped out of the plane with no injuries, except of course to his pride!

You may not desire to fly an airplane, but people other than pilots fly solo. Salespeople go out alone to call on clients, entrepreneurs start new businesses by themselves, and pastors lead churches without other pastoral (professional) help. And just like with flying an airplane, if you want to pastor a church solo, it's best to take lessons first.

Pastoral training comes in many forms. An aspiring pastor often attends school—Bible school, college, university, seminary—to learn the basics of Bible study, sermon preparation, pastoral care, and other aspects of pastoral ministry. The tradition of learning lessons in a class setting has a long history going back to Elijah and his school of prophets. Throughout the centuries, training has gone through numerous iterations and is commonly required for entry into pastoral ministry in denominations and associations of churches. While some church groups require pastors to have an academic degree, others are happy to appoint or call those who demonstrate just a clear call to ministry, with training taking place on the job or through mentoring by more experienced pastors. It's common for pastors in such groups to experience a call to ministry and jump in with no training (or very little). In any case, no person is ever trained to be a pastor by getting a degree. Pastoral training is an ongoing process that happens through practice and life experience.

10

Whatever level of training a potential pastor obtains, it never seems to be enough. Allow me to use myself as an example. I look back at my ministry experience beginning in high school. As the student leader of my church's youth group, I had the opportunity to teach, preach, and guide the group. In college I served as a youth pastor in two different churches and worked for a year as a pastoral assistant in another church before graduating with a BA in biblical studies. While in seminary, I served four years as a Christian education pastor. After graduating with my MDiv, I felt I was ready to be the lead pastor of a church. There weren't many job opportunities that year for recent seminary graduates, but a friend recommended me to a congregation who called me to be their pastor. Since I had no other offers, I decided it would be a good place to start, since I'd be preaching and teaching on a regular basis. I assumed my years of experience in church ministry were sufficient for me to lead the church, even though I was the solo pastor.

It took just a few months for me to realize I was in trouble. While seminary provided a fine education (I was doing my own translation from the Greek for my sermons like my professors had taught me), it didn't prepare me for pastoring alone. The church was influenced by two families who comprised one-third of the congregation. No one in my college or seminary training had alerted me about family-controlled churches, but I learned quickly that they did not really desire for their church to grow. (Who needs new people, right? Why, they might even want to take over.) It was evident they had called me not to lead them but rather to do what they wished: mow the lawn, clean the toilets, prepare the bulletin, run errands, open and close the building, visit everyone, care for the elderly, be on call at all hours, and run the church office. In their view, I was a hired hand and their personal chaplain. I discovered that leading a church as a solo pastor was challenging.

While sizable congregations with media visibility make it appear that churches operate with a large staff, a significant number of churches are led by solo pastors. My research has found that most church denominations or associations don't track the total number of churches pastored by a single person. However, "Religious Congregations in 21st Century America," a National Congregations Study, reported that 56 percent of Protestant churches in the United States are led by solo pastors.[1] Some denominations or church families are almost exclusively made up of churches led by solo pastors. For example, Village Missions, a ministry providing pastors to churches located in smaller communities, reports that 95 percent of its pastors serve alone. Various ethnic churches are also predominantly led by solo pastors, reporting between 90 to 95 percent solo pastors. Larger denominations report more churches with multiple pastors, but the Assemblies of God reports 43 percent, the Southern Baptist Convention reports 66 percent, and the Wesleyan Church reports 67 percent of their pastors soloing. A personal email inquiry of church leaders revealed that 77 percent of their churches are pastored by a single person.[2] Thus, it appears that on average between 60 to 77 percent of churches in the United States are led by solo pastors, a significantly large number.

These solo pastors face challenges related to feelings of loneliness, a lack of resources, poor administration, little respect, limited vision, personal conflict, struggles for control, pressures of preaching, tight finances, managing misconceptions, dealing with the poor, and a host of other issues. Like soloing in an airplane, leading a church alone has its exciting moments, but many solo pastors end up crashing like my friend. Some are not as fortunate as he was to do so without injury, which is why I've written this book.

The Solo Pastor is inspired by my forty-seven years of ministry involvement as a pastor, consultant, and professor. For thirty-seven years, I've served as a seminary professor at Talbot School of Theology, training pastors for local church ministry. My estimate is that 85 percent of my students who went on to preaching ministry initially served as solo pastors. Throughout my ministry career,

I've engaged in numerous conversations with solo pastors, listening to their stories of victory and defeat. This book is a product of those years.

The Solo Pastor is written specifically for the solo pastor serving a single-staff church. It articulates the major challenges of pastoring a church alone and provides practical help so solo pastors can lead their churches fruitfully. Each chapter begins with an imaginary conversation involving Pastors Bill Collier and Jim Hunter. You may be tempted to skip over these introductory sections, but I recommend that you resist such temptation. While the conversations are fictitious, they are based on conversations I've had with actual solo pastors in real-life situations. Each conversation sets up the remainder of the chapter, and I'm certain you'll identify with many, if not most, of the situations. Throughout the book, comments made by solo pastors are used without identifying them. Most shared their stories confidentially. I appreciate each pastor's openness in sharing their perspectives and struggles. Thus, I've honored their wishes to remain anonymous.

So, you are going to pastor (or are pastoring) a church alone? Let me tell you a secret. It's more challenging than you might expect. But with training and the insights obtained from those who have flown the course before you, you'll have a great opportunity to succeed in making disciples in your church.

Gary L. McIntosh,
Temecula, California

PART 1

The Solo Pastor
Learns to Fly

ONE

Go Solo

The average pastor's job is harder than average.

—Lyle E. Schaller

Pastor Bill Collier's first few months at Faith Church were uneventful. People seemed to appreciate his sermons and the humor he often used to illustrate his points. His attempts to organize the church to plan for the coming year were welcomed. Members told him confidentially that the former pastor was a caring person but never did much planning. Over time the congregation became frustrated with the lack of long-range vision and gently prayed the pastor out. They then intentionally sought out a new pastor who had better skills at leading and managing the congregation. Since Pastor Collier met their new criteria, he was the one they called. Everyone appeared pleased with the early progress.

That's why Pastor Collier wasn't concerned when the matriarch of the church asked for an appointment. Following a few pleasantries, Mary got directly to the reason for her visit. "Pastor . . ." She spoke with a slight tremor in her voice. "You don't love people."

"I don't understand," Pastor Collier replied, his eyebrows lifted in shock.

"Well, you haven't visited my mother in two months. Our last pastor visited her every week."

Swallowing hard, Pastor Collier tried to explain that his gifts were more along the lines of leading and managing the church rather than pastoral care. He added, "As you'll recall, when the church voted to call me, they asked that I focus my efforts on moving the church forward in renewed growth."

"I remember," Mary agreed, "but I didn't think you'd neglect the older folks."

THIS IMAGINARY CONVERSATION may sound familiar. It illustrates the challenges often faced by solo pastors in single-staff churches. Pastorates that begin with sweet excitement turn sour when people express disappointment that the minister is not meeting their expectations. Pastors often put on a proverbial poker face and pretend the words don't hurt, but deep below the surface it stings.

Serving as a solo pastor is a demanding role for a number of reasons. In my conversations with solo pastors, the following reasons surface most often.

1. Solo pastors wear numerous ministry hats.

As the only trained ministry leader, solo pastors regularly serve as the key leader for most ministries. One pastor told me, "When I was the pastor of a fifty-member church in western Nebraska, I was the senior pastor, youth director, Awana commander, VBS director, worship leader, small group coordinator, primary adult Sunday school teacher, men's group leader, and church grounds-keeper. As the senior pastor/shepherd, I was responsible for all the things that most senior pastors do, such as preaching, counseling, visitation, leading, etc. I eventually handed several of these hats over to church members, but there were reasons why I needed to take them on for a while."

2. Solo pastors rarely get a break.

"The weekly weight of preaching can be crazy with extra hospital visits, funerals, community events, etc.," wrote a pastor from Arizona. "It would be nice once in a while to be able to look to an associate pastor to fill the pulpit for me, but this is not available. No matter the week, every week, I must preach, which almost always is a joy, but sometimes I wish there was an occasional break." Over time, the reality of being on call 24/7 wears on most solo pastors. The pressure to work on their scheduled day off or even to skip vacations weighs heavy. For some, the only way to get a break is to change churches or leave ministry for another job.

3. Solo pastors are required to serve in areas of personal weakness and for which they have little passion.

As the opening conversation of this chapter illustrates, a pastor who is skilled in pastoral care is normally not as skilled in organizational management; the one skilled in organizational management is normally not as skilled in pastoral care. A solo pastor must do counseling even when that's not their gift. They must manage the church's budget even when they have trouble balancing their own checkbook. Most pastors are not skilled at or passionate about every ministry in a church. The natural tendency is for a pastor to gravitate toward the ministries that invigorate them while letting other ministries languish. This fact shows up every time a new pastor is called or appointed, when the pendulum of gifts and passion swings opposite of the pastor who departs. "Being a solo pastor, I have to do a lot of different things in running the church, and plenty of them are outside my area of gifting," wrote a pastor from Maine. "So church paperwork and other office work pull me away from study, visiting people, discipling, and leadership building."

4. Solo pastors are usually underpaid, with few if any benefits.
Low pay and few benefits require some solo pastors to become bivocational, working second jobs to make financial ends meet. For example, a pastor shared that he is considered full-time by his church, but he is paid slightly over minimum wage. He has no health insurance, retirement funding, or ministry expense account of any kind. Everything his family needs comes out of his personal account. To compensate, he drives a school bus and works as a salesman when school is not in session. This bivocational lifestyle hurts the entire church by minimizing the full impact he could have in leading the church to make disciples. Exceptions can be found, but it's rare for bivocational pastors to lead growing churches.

5. Solo pastors are normally envisioned as caretakers and caregivers by the congregation.
A solo pastor's primary role is defined before they even arrive at a church to begin ministry. Certain ministerial expectations are already at play in people's minds. This is true even when a congregation gives a pastor clear instructions to move in a new or renewed direction. The pastor's desire to work outside certain parameters eventually leads to dissatisfaction, trouble, and conflict. "People grow frustrated that you have not visited them in their home for a while," communicated a middle-aged pastor. "In a solo-pastor church, people often expect regular pastoral contact, even though others care for them too."

Solo pastors are left to deal with caretaking issues by themselves that are unseen by the congregation. For example, dealing with the poor. In larger churches with multiple staff, when someone in the community calls or comes to the church for financial assistance, a secretary or associate staff person handles the situation according to church policy. Not so with a solo pastor. As one pastor pointed out, "As the solo pastor whose office is in the house, people call or come to my doorstep directly, and regularly. It's an interruption to the workday and an emotional weight to carry. When people are on your doorstep literally crying because they can't pay their $200 electric bill, and per church policy all you can do is give them $50 on a one-time basis up to one incident per month, it's emotionally tough. Or, if they are chronic abusers and you tell them that you can't help them at this time, and they start yelling at you that you are unloving. Well, it's hard to close the door after they leave and resume working on your sermon."

6. *Solo pastors are lonely.*

Though solo pastors can and do build close relationships with people in their churches, the relationships tend to center around church ministry and family life. Solo pastors must carefully navigate conversations with church folk and typically avoid deep discussions about ministry trials and challenges. It's not really possible to talk shop since parishioners don't understand the weight of expectations pastors carry. If a solo pastor doesn't intentionally build relationships outside the church, particularly with other like-minded pastors, they can become extremely lonely.

Highly driven solo pastors may not be able to develop relationships easily. Others may need to be away from larger groups of people so they can recharge, a fact not well accepted by some in the congregation. One pastor wrote, "Not having other pastors/elders in the flock can be lonely. It adds a higher level of vulnerability, as things go better in the context of many equal counselors. I think, too, this causes me to share more with my spouse than she needs to hear, which leads to more stress at home."

7. *Solo pastors navigate unwritten rules alone.*

The inner workings of a church are well-known by the long-term members and attendees—that is, almost everyone but the solo pastor. As loving and welcoming as a congregation may be, the reality is that the pastor (particularly a new pastor) is an outsider who is not in the know. No one tells the solo pastor the internal tacit rules until they violate one of them. Take Pastor Randy (not

> *Pastoring is increasingly like coaching pro football: Being under pressure is part of the territory.*
>
> —*Kevin Miller*

his real name), for example. Pastor Randy was told by the elders of his church to be himself. They assured him that they desired him to be authentic in every way, whether teaching, socializing, or leading. Soon after his arrival, Randy attended a dinner for young couples at the home of one of the elders. When it came time for dessert, a tray of cookies was passed around the table. When the tray reached Pastor Randy, the elder, who was sitting at the opposite end of the table of twelve people, called out, "Hey Pastor, throw me a cookie." Pastor Randy knew the elder didn't mean it literally, but being in a playful mood, he picked up a cookie and tossed it to the man. Everyone laughed at the time. Later, after everyone had left, the elder berated Pastor Randy for throwing a cookie in his home. Randy discovered that you can be your authentic self, except when you can't.

8. Solo pastors lead churches that are resource poor.

Solo pastors are faced with leveraging limited resources for the greatest impact. This becomes a point of conflict when the pastor's vision and ideas do not match the long-standing mores of a church that is oriented toward self-preservation rather than outreach and growth. Solo pastors are afraid to ask for what they need. They need a raise but are afraid to ask. They need help but are afraid to ask. They need time off but are afraid to ask. "For a single-pastor church, finances are often tight. My church recently adopted a safety policy and safety team to deal with CPR, first aid, and active shooters," recalled one solo pastor. "A larger church would hire and pay for a professional consultant or attorney, but as a solo pastor, I and another layperson set our hand to drafting/

writing this policy. It involved hours of time that was not directly shepherding people."

9. Solo pastors deal with the church's primary influential person, couple, or family with no support.

Churches that have existed for a decade or longer are influenced by intergenerational families or couples. In most cases these people are godly individuals who have served as the core of the church for a long time. Stories abound, however, of key families controlling churches in negative ways. People in such congregations may want the pastor to stand up to these powerful families, but few will side with the pastor for the sake of keeping the peace and the status quo. After all, pastors come and go, but influential families stay, and congregants will need to live with them in harmony for years to come. Powerful families are not always on the church board or in ministry positions, which may keep them undercover for a time. In some situations, all the people in a congregation are related through marriage or have long-term relationships, making their control even stronger and more difficult to circumvent.

10. Solo pastors struggle to embrace the nonchurched community.

The reasons for this are complex but boil down to the solo pastor being (1) too busy, (2) a first-time pastor with little experience, (3) a pastor whose primary gifts are shepherding, caregiving, and counseling, (4) overwhelmed with just keeping the church afloat, and/or (5) insecure about ministry philosophy and approach. Related to this is the lack of a clear way to handle controversial issues like abortion, gay rights, racial diversity, and political differences. A solo pastor can't lead a smaller church to address all or even a few of the major issues. They just don't have the emotional bandwidth or resources to do so. "I feel foggy on what I should or shouldn't do in the cultural thought war," commented one solo pastor. "I really don't see the apostle Paul bothering with social injustice, but I also see where the William Wilberforces of the church made great strides in uprooting social injustice."

11. Solo pastors do not receive special training that might allow them to be fruitful.

Few solo pastors have learned to think missiologically, ethnographically, or geographically about the church or its ministry area. Dissonance between urban, suburban, and rural communities and between small-church, medium-church, and large-church approaches to ministry is unexplored, misunderstood, or unknown. Solo pastors serve churches located in different settings—rural, inner city, suburban, urban—where each environment has a unique set of circumstances and difficulties.

12. Solo pastors are more insecure than they appear.

Congregants see their pastor as confident, and pastors appear so. Their exterior appearance, unfortunately, doesn't always match their fragile interior. Those who are the most insecure are the most resistant to sharing their feelings with others. They're simply too insecure to do so. Others honestly feel like they don't know what they're doing. Overwhelmed by the multiple models and choices of how to do ministry today, some solo pastors freeze up. They become indecisive and overly cautious, leading to poor leadership. Dealing with the intangibles of ministry is difficult. The brain work, people work, organizational work, conflict work, and discipleship work have no definite answers. Plus, ministry is never over. A good sermon this Sunday is wonderful, but next Sunday is coming fast. Managing one conflictive situation this week is heartening, but another conflict is on the horizon.

13. Solo pastors struggle at home.

One pastor wrote, "The simple truth is what we post on Facebook and Instagram is not always true. There are no perfect marriages—not yours, not mine, and not your pastor's." Most of the challenges already noted impact the solo pastor's family in negative ways. A pastor's wife and children experience the aftermath of dealing with power brokers in the church, the anxiety of a low income, and the loneliness due to a lack of friendships, among other things, much of which leads to unhealthy stress on the entire family.

14. Solo pastors struggle with being compared to pastors of larger churches.

Everyone has access to the best preachers and church leaders each week via the internet, television, or podcasts. Comparisons may be unfair, but they are inevitable. A solo pastor's insecurity is exacerbated by peers serving larger churches. Although other pastors would never say it out loud, their thinking is that if you were any good, you'd be at a larger church.

Even in situations where the pastors of larger churches are supportive, solo pastors may lose members to them due to the larger menu of services provided. "I find that a lot of solo pastors deal with the negative emotions associated with the feeder-receptor phenomenon where the small church attracts the unbeliever, nurtures them to Christ, and loses them to the larger church that has more programs to offer," related a frustrated solo pastor. "I worked for two, maybe three, years to win and disciple a family. They attended my church for about a year before telling me they were going to start attending the nearby megachurch, since it offered a wider assortment of ministry for their children. It broke my heart. I have nothing against this megachurch or its pastor. He's always been encouraging and supportive whenever I've met him. It still hurts deeply when people leave my church for his, especially after I've worked so hard to reach them." There was a time when solo pastors were respected and appreciated, but the growing size gaps between churches lead solo pastors to feel like failures.

15. Solo pastors deal with misconceptions.

While all pastors deal with misconceptions, "sometimes people in a solo-pastor church who disagree with you will charge you with being a dictator. It's easy for that to happen when people see the leadership not as a team but as a solo leader," recalled one solo pastor. "This misconception impacts the spiritual formation of church members too. Christianity in the United States is very much an individual enterprise. By this I'm not advocating pastoral dictatorship. Certainly, pastors can abuse their authority. But I think the pendulum is way too lopsided in the other direction, as the elders have almost no authority to direct the moral and behavioral lives of the congregation."

16. *Solo pastors own church ministry more than others in the church.*

"I do make a real effort to delegate things," explained a solo pastor, "and involve the body in the work of the ministry. So often, of course, folks don't own the ministry like I do, and these delegated posts wind up back on my desk. For example, I had a children's teacher, but their family desired to travel for months at a time. They'd just leave with no thought of finding a replacement for themselves. It all falls back onto my desk, causing me to scramble to fill the teaching posts. People are casual about their commitments and don't communicate well if they are not going to be there."

17. *The work of solo pastors is never done.*

One of the best ways to describe a church pastored by a solo pastor is as a garden. Producing a nice garden takes a lot of sequenced work—tilling, planting, watering, weeding, and harvesting. If the soil is good and the gardener puts in the effort, the garden produces good fruit. It is, however, hard work, and the work is never done. If the soil is bad, the garden is not as fruitful, but the work is still hard and never done.

> *Pastors don't get paid much, but you can't beat the hours.*
>
> —*An anonymous church member*

In an email, one solo pastor confirmed, "It's tough being a solo pastor. I currently am sitting here alone in a local restaurant with tears in my eyes from not knowing what to do next. I want to be the best pastor I can here. At times I simply don't know how to do that based on what I feel the limitations are in my current church. There are so many random expectations of me as the pastor. Ironically, I don't know whose expectations to use as my litmus test for being a successful pastor here. It seems as if each group—elders, deacons, teachers, workers—has a different understanding of my role."

THE SOLO-PASTOR CHURCH has always been the primary type of church, and it's likely to remain so in the future. Difficult financial realities throughout the United States, as well as around the world, mean that more and more churches will be led by a single paid staff member rather than a full professional staff. Leading a church as the only staff person is difficult, as this chapter has shown. Therefore, it is important to prepare to lead a church alone. Understanding solo churches, how they operate and function, is a good place to begin. The service of solo pastors is no less important to God than the service of pastors employed by churches with multiple staff members.

— THREE QUESTIONS

1. Pastor Collier's story is just one of many stories that could be told. What is your story?
2. Which of the demands on solo pastors have you personally experienced?
3. What would you add to the list?

— TWO IDEAS

1. Using your own words, make a list of the challenges you face as a solo pastor in a single-staff church today.
2. Rank the list, with the most challenging aspects first, second, and so forth.

TWO

Understand Solo Churches

The personality of the church usually determines the type of leadership that is effective.

—D. G. McCoury

I accepted an appointment to this church because I thought the people wanted me to lead," declared Bill Collier, the thirty-five-year-old pastor of Faith Church. "When I interviewed for the position, they said they wanted three things from me. First, to preach the Word of God. Second, to lead them in developing a new vision for the future. Third, to reach the community for Christ."

"That all sounds pretty good to me," responded his longtime friend and fellow pastor Jim Hunter. "But you sound a bit upset. Am I hearing you right?"

"Yes, I guess you are," admitted Bill. "I try to disguise my frustration when I'm with the members of my church. It's nice to be able to talk openly with you, though."

"That's what friends are for," responded the older pastor.

"Thanks. I appreciate you taking time for me today." Bill looked away from Jim as he continued. "I've tried to lead the church to develop a vision for reaching the lost and growing a great church, but they don't seem committed to that idea at all. They don't want to take any risks and honestly are happy if I just focus all my attention on them and their needs."

"I can see how that would be frustrating, Bill. But that's how churches with a solo pastor are wired."

"What do you mean?" asked Bill. "I don't understand."

"Think of it this way," Jim suggested. "You can view the church as either a family or an army. Both ideas are used as metaphors in the Bible for the church. Take, for instance, Acts 2:41–47, where a description of the early church is given. Luke describes the church as being together, having all things in common, breaking bread, meeting from house to house, and being committed to the apostles' teaching, to fellowship, and to prayer. It all sounds pretty much like a family gathering."

"I can see that for sure," Bill agreed. "It sounds like my extended family when we get together on a holiday."

"It sure does," Jim concurred. "So, what's really important to your family?"

"Right offhand, I'd say it's important that we love and care for each other. And that we accept each other just as we are, warts and all."

"Right!" Jim raised his voice. "And who receives the largest measure of care?"

"Hmm," Bill pondered. "I'd say it's the children and the oldest members of the family. We always prepare a special table for the children. Everyone makes a fuss over how tall the children have grown, stuff like that. And of course we always take care to help the older members of our family get safely from the cars into the house to comfortable seats."

"Of course you do," Jim confirmed. "Have you ever had times of disagreement at family gatherings?"

"Certainly, but it's not much fun. I'd say we go out of our way to minimize disagreements. We really want to have fun together rather than argue."

"Right. You want an environment of safety, security, and peace. Now, here's one more question," Jim said as he motioned with one finger in the air. "If I desired to become a member of your family, how would I do it?"

"I've never given that much thought. I guess you could marry my sister." Bill chuckled.

"I'm already spoken for," Jim said with a laugh. "What other ways could I join your family?"

"I could adopt you." Bill smiled. "My youngest niece is adopted, so that's another way in. You could also be born into our family, but I think it's a little too late for that to happen."

"More than a little late, I think." Jim snickered. "Now, all that you've mentioned is very much like churches with solo pastors. The highest values are love, care, and acceptance. The key people are the children and the elderly. People want safety, security, and peace. And the way the church grows is through the addition of new people who are birthed, adopted, or married into the family."

"I've never thought of a church this way before. It does make sense. I guess that's why the members of my church want me to focus on pastoral care rather than outreach. Am I correct?" Bill asked.

"Yes, you are. If you provide love and care for everyone, especially the weaker members of the family—children and elderly—then the people get what they really desire—safety, security, and peace—and you'll be called a faithful pastor. A solo pastor's faithfulness is regularly judged by the way they care for these vulnerable members."

"What you're saying is that the people in my church honestly didn't call me to be their visionary leader but to be their caregiver and protector?"

> *The pastor must build a relationship of trust, not only with elected church leaders, but also with the opinion makers, those who wield influence through the informal power structure of the congregation.*
>
> —D. G. McCoury

"You've got it," Jim said. "However, you still lead, but through personal relationships focused on caring. You see, the solo-pastor church grows as the family reaches out to those in their network of friends, family, and associates. Yet their desire for safety, security, and peace often keeps them from taking risks that might help the church grow, even though the risks might be reasonable. What's really desired in a pastor is someone who can help them build a strong community."

"That's my church in a proverbial nutshell." Bill sighed.

"In contrast to a family, think of an army. We don't readily think of the church as an army, but several passages of Scripture suggest this as a metaphor. The first time Jesus mentions the church in Matthew 16:18, he promises its growth. He says he will build his church, 'and the gates of Hades will not overpower it.'"

"I've preached on that passage several times," Bill commented.

"Me too. I used to understand that image as the church in a defensive posture. Then a few years ago it dawned on me that gates are a defensive weapon, not an offensive weapon. The picture in this passage is of the church moving forward, and Satan in a defensive position. The church is like an army moving forward against the enemy."

"Wow. I've never seen that before," Bill admitted.

"I hadn't either. But here's the point: large multi-staff churches think more like an army than a family."

"How so?" Bill inquired.

"As I see it," Jim continued, "the major values of an army are loyalty, commitment, and a willingness to take risks, sometimes extreme risks for the cause. Love and care for the soldiers are important but not the core values. Thus, instead of the key persons being the weakest members, like children and the elderly are in a family, the key people in an army are the highly committed and the risk-takers. Then, too, consider how a person becomes part of an army. One gets into an army by signing up, joining, or enlisting, sometimes even being drafted."

"Okay, I see the difference," Bill noted.

"The leader's job in an army," Jim continued, "is not to create a community that values love, care, and acceptance but rather to create a fighting force willing to take risks for the cause, whatever it is. To motivate soldiers, the leader focuses on challenging people to fulfill a great vision, but in a family, the motivation comes from challenging people to create an environment of safety, security, and peace."

"Okay. Let me see if I understand what you're saying. A single-staff church is like a family, where the establishing of community is the key goal, while the multi-staff church is like an army, where fulfilling the cause is the key goal. Is that right?"

"That's a good summary." Jim nodded as he tore a piece of paper out of his notebook. "It'd be something like this."

	SINGLE-STAFF CHURCH	MULTI-STAFF CHURCH
Metaphor	Family	Army
Values	Love, care, acceptance	Loyalty, commitment, risk
Key People	Children and elderly	Highly committed and risk-takers
Entrance	Born, adopted, marry into	Sign up, enlist, join
Motivation	Safety, security, peace	Vision

It took Jim a few moments to write out his summary chart. Laying down his pen, he looked up at Bill and continued, "There are always two tensions in a solo-pastor church: nurture and outreach.

Without some evangelistic outreach, the church loses people, becoming ever smaller. Yet the question people always ask is 'What are you doing for me and my family?'"

"Yeah. Shocking. Tell me something I didn't already know." Bill smirked.

"Without effort toward outreach, nurture always wins in the solo-pastor church."

"Right," Bill confirmed.

"Outreach is determined by two things: size of the church and context. In a smaller solo-pastor church, outreach must be focused on providing love and care for others. Since the people already in the church value love, care, and acceptance, it's necessary to turn those values toward people outside the church. Preaching and sharing the gospel become effective when wrapped in those values," Jim advised. "Second is context. If you're in an area with lots of middle-class families, the church may find fruitfulness with outreach through family-oriented sports programs. If your church is in an area with major poverty and injustice, you'll find more success with outreach ministry targeted toward assisting the poor. Putting those two dynamics together, a solo-pastor church must target its outreach to the needs of the community—context—but always through some type of ministry that offers some aspect of love and care." Jim looked back to his sheet of paper as he finished speaking.

"Okay. I'm getting the picture," Bill said. "If my church is in a rural, urban, modern, postmodern, monocultural, or multicultural context, it has to adapt, but it still must highlight the values of love, care, and acceptance. Right?"

Jim nodded.

"I guess outreach isn't simple. I need to open my Bible and my news apps, as well as my mind and heart, to wrestle with God on how to reach my community."

Jim nodded again. "You're tracking with me," he said. "You see, the basic questions on people's minds in a solo-pastor church are 'Do you love us? Do you really love us? Will you always love us?' So, when you try to lead them, it must be done in the midst of secure love. If it isn't, outreach will fail."

"I think you've lost me there," Bill confessed.

"Maybe this story will help. After exploring the context of his church, another pastor friend of mine led his church to start a basketball league to reach the elementary children in the neighborhood around the church building. There was a man in the church who had a love for kids and basketball as well as for sharing the gospel. He took over the direction of the league and spent many evenings getting to know the children who participated in the league and their parents. In time he even led some of them to Christ. As more people came to Christ, the pastor excitedly spent more and more time with the new people. One day a longtime couple in the church emailed him and asked him to drop by in the afternoon. After sharing some pleasantries, the couple announced they were leaving the church. Stunned, he asked why, to which they replied, 'Because you love people outside the church more than those inside the church.' What I'm saying about the solo-pastor church is that the values of love, care, and acceptance are so strong that you must never neglect them or create a situation where people feel you've forgotten them."

"So, the key ingredient in the solo-pastor church is love?" Bill asked.

"Correctamundo." Jim nodded again.

"So, I think I get the picture now," Bill asserted. "My church is a family that values love, care, and acceptance. Our vision will need to be about sharing the love we have for one another with those outside the church. If I'm to lead them to grow into a healthier body, I'll need to go about it as a family would—that is, caring for the current family members while celebrating the newcomers as new additions to the family."

"There's more to it, of course, but that's the basic core," Jim concurred.

THIS EXTENDED CONVERSATION highlights what is perhaps the core aspect of a solo-pastor church. As Jim notes, however, there's a lot more to it. Here are additional aspects of solo-pastor churches that are worth considering.

1. Authority and power are not what they appear.

Leadership influence in a solo-pastor church is like an iceberg. Formal authority is the tip of the iceberg that is visible above the waterline, and informal power is what is not seen below the waterline. The church's formal organizational structure is the 13 percent above the surface, while the informal network of complex relationships is the 87 percent below the surface. The important thing to realize is that the real power lies submerged below the waterline.

Authority is a matter of structure—church polity, organizational charts, titles—but power is a matter of sociological dynamics—relationships, traditions, history. Solo-pastor churches follow a historic pattern of authority and power, whereby the solo pastor may have authority but rarely the power. The true leaders in the church are the longtime faithful members, usually a family or network of a few families and individuals. This traditional pattern of authority and power continues unless a catastrophic event takes place, such as a part of the church building catching fire, a death of a key member, or a church conflict that causes a churchwide restructuring of aptitudes and expectations. It is therefore wise for a solo pastor to understand and work with this pattern before attempting any major changes in the church.

2. Solo-pastor churches want their pastor to care for them more than to lead them.

Assuming the solo-pastor church has been around for over a decade, it's likely the congregation desires a pastor to care for them rather than to lead them. Their deep desire is for the pastor to serve as a personal chaplain, much like royalty in bygone days in Europe employed their own personal chaplains to serve their needs. This understanding of the solo pastor's role is held tightly but can be changed over time through the steady teaching and modeling of the pastor or through a major event as previously mentioned.

The expectation that a solo pastor be a caregiver is true no matter what the congregation says when seeking a new pastor. During an interview, church leaders may say a number of nice-sounding words to attract a pastor. For instance, commonly stated desires are for strong leadership, fresh vision for the future, evangelistic outreach, attracting newcomers, and a willingness to change to reach the younger generation. For the most part, such desires are swallowed in their entirety by the prospective pastor but prove illusive once the pastor is installed.

3. Solo pastors can and do lead.

While they may not have power, solo pastors can lead through personal influence. A solo pastor may need to give sacrificial care to church members for a time, but in doing so they can put Ephesians 4:11–12 into practice to equip others for ministry. They may have less formal power than they wish, but they have more influence than they may realize. Conversations in meetings, casual gatherings, and informal visits are opportunities to create tension around needs, cast vision, and create times of change. A simple policy of taking others along on ministry assignments—for example, the solo pastor asking other church leaders to accompany them on hospital visits—can serve to equip others for the work of ministry, even as others don't realize they're being trained.

4. Preaching gives the solo pastor influence over the entire congregation.

In discussions regarding authority, power, and influence, it's easy to forget that the solo pastor is at the center of communication through their pulpit ministry. When a pastor effectively communicates to the congregation what the church is about, one of two things will happen over time: either the church will get rid of the pastor, or the pastor will gather around themselves people who share their perspective on the future of the church. It will take around six to seven years of faithful preaching, teaching, and modeling for the second to happen, but it will happen.

The ability to watch and listen to the best preachers in the world via the internet has raised the expectations of people in solo-pastor churches for better sermons. However, people in solo-pastor churches remain forgiving of less than stellar sermons—if they feel loved and cared for. Of course, the better a communicator the solo pastor is, the stronger their position as a leader. Thus, it is sensible for a solo pastor to work at improving their communication skills.

5. *People in solo-pastor churches desire church growth to a point.*

People in solo-pastor churches become sensitive to the need for growth when they see their church at a danger point of decline. At that point, they almost magically become interested in outreach and growth. They'll continue to desire, encourage, and support growth until the church reaches a point of financial and numerical stability. Once the church is restored to a point of viability, their interest in church growth declines.

The truth is people don't want the church to grow; they just don't want it to die. The solo pastor needs to be aware of this dynamic as they act on the opportunity to wisely institute changes and a new direction.

6. *Solo pastors must live with tension and ambiguity.*

People will desire good preaching *and* good care, church growth *and* church health, effective outreach *and* effective in-reach. Accomplishing both aspects at the same time is difficult. Solo pastors must balance outreach to unchurched people with caring for current church members, spending time in sermon preparation with visiting those in the church family, and dreaming great dreams for the future with managing church business.

7. Solo pastors must accept the roles of initiator and catalyst.
It takes new ministries and programs to reach new people. The fact is if people were attracted to the ministries the solo-pastor church already has in place, they'd already be in the church. Since they're not and are not likely to come, new ministries are needed to reach them. It's highly unlikely that the long-term members will start anything new, which means the solo pastor must accept the roles of initiator and catalyst if the church is to become effective in outreach.

8. Solo-pastor churches have sacred programs, sacred places, sacred people, and sacred secrets.
The difficulty is that these sacred things are not communicated to solo pastors, who must discover them on their own. This causes friction as the solo pastor mistakenly intrudes into the sacred without any awareness of doing anything wrong. As a family, the church is bonded together by everything that is sacred to it, and attempts at beginning new ministries, assigning new leaders or workers, and changing old formats and forms of church life are viewed as unnecessary change at the minimum and dangerous at the maximum. Among other things, this means that a solo-pastor church finds it easiest to get on board with a vision that is consistent with its heritage. For example, if a church has a tradition of children's ministry, a new vision that involves reaching children is more likely to be accepted than one, say, that focuses on teaching singles.

> *Don't butcher sacred cows. People will not follow us if they sense we're trying to rustle their sacred cows.*
>
> *—Ben Patterson*

— THREE QUESTIONS

1. Does your understanding of the solo-pastor church align with that described by Pastor Jim Hunter in the opening section of this chapter? Why or why not?
2. In what ways has the solo-pastor church created frustration for you personally? Give two or three examples.
3. What insights could you add to this chapter?

— TWO IDEAS

1. Make a list of the pastors who served the church before you came and find out as much as possible about their ministries. Then ask: How long did each one stay? What challenges did they face? What impact did they have on the church? What insights can I gain from their experiences?
2. Construct a picture of your church's power structure by drawing an iceberg on a sheet of paper. Write the names of the people in your church on the iceberg, with the names of the most influential people below the waterline, and the least influential above the waterline. Who has the most power in your church and why? How might this drawing inform your ministry in this church?

THREE

Explore
Solo Leadership

A large church wants a pastor who leads them; a small church wants
a pastor they can lead.

—Lyle E. Schaller

How did your last board meeting go?" Jim inquired as he slid
into the booth at Sally's Restaurant.

"Okay," Bill responded while simultaneously adjusting the sil-
verware on the table. "I guess things went well."

"You sound a bit unsure."

"It was more than a bit exasperating. I tried leading the board
to set a vision for the next ten years, but it didn't really go over
as I expected."

"Tell me more."

"I remember taking a class in seminary on leadership. My
professor shared that the new theory of leadership was called

transformational leadership. The basic idea is that a leader brings change to their situation by casting a vision for the future and then guiding people to accomplish it. So, I asked my board members to think about where they wished our church to be in ten years. You know . . . to help them begin creating a vision."

Jim glanced up from looking at the breakfast menu. "So, what did they say?"

"They couldn't think of a single thing." Bill sighed. "After a few minutes of hearing nothing from them, I asked where they wanted the church to be in five years. The board members still couldn't come up with anything. It was crazy. Finally, out of frustration, I asked, 'Where do you want the church to be next year?' Finally! Finally, they came up with some ideas. Honestly, it was extremely frustrating. How am I to lead this church toward renewal if my key leaders can't envision a better future?"

"Remember our conversation from last month," Jim began, "the one where I talked about a smaller church being like a family?"

"I do."

"Think back to that conversation and consider how it applies to leading your church. Given the size and context of your church, what might be the best way to lead board members to catch a renewed vision for the future?"

"I haven't given it much thought, but maybe by loving and caring for them? Is that what you're getting at?"

"You're heading in the right direction," Jim affirmed. "I think the way you were trying to lead the board was more like what might be done in a larger church. Larger churches expect the pastor to lead them from the stage. Solo-pastor churches expect pastors to lead them from the floor."

"What do you mean?" Bill questioned with a puzzled tone.

"Have you heard the cliché 'People don't care what you know until they know you care'?"

"Yes."

"It's honestly true, especially in a solo-pastor church. As the solo pastor, you are the chaplain or caregiver of the people. Therefore, your ministry is primarily one of presence—that is, being present at gatherings, births, deaths, baptisms, weddings, nursing homes, hospitals, and other events. Leading as a solo pastor is like walking beside people as a spiritual chaplain."

"I know we have to marry, bury, and baptize people, but shouldn't we be making some disciples along the way? Shouldn't we be leading the church to a better future?"

"Certainly," Jim agreed, "but I'm suggesting that *how* to do that is from within a loving and caring relationship rather than from the platform or, in your recent case, from the head of the boardroom table. The key is to remember that your church thinks of leadership in terms of relationships rather than in terms of transformative vision. As a solo pastor, you must always recognize the primacy of relationship. Any project, program, or activity is judged by how it will impact relationships."

"That makes a great deal of sense," Bill admitted. "In my excitement to develop a vision, maybe I put the proverbial cart before the horse." He chuckled. "My wife tells me I tend to do that quite often."

"Our spouses know us pretty well," Jim acknowledged. "I know mine certainly does."

"I remember reading a book about the life of the legendary basketball coach John Wooden," Bill continued. "It told how he always focused on the basics in practice. I know the essentials for basketball are dribbling, shooting, passing, rebounding, and defending, but what are they for leading as a solo pastor?"

IT'S A GREAT QUESTION. What are the basics of leading as a solo pastor? As this conversation reveals, leading as a solo pastor is challenging. Here are some insights and tips to help you improve your leadership as a solo pastor.

1. People will buy into you before they buy into your vision.

If you are a solo pastor, your ability to establish relationships with people in the church is more important than your ability to manage budgets, start new programs, or develop and carry out a vision for future growth. Through the close scrutiny of face-to-face relationships, people discover your true character. Your fruitfulness will hinge on people seeing you as a genuine person who cares about others. As they buy into you, trusting you, they will buy into your vision for the future of their church.

Vision is caught, not taught. Leading effectively happens through trusting relationships in a solo-pastor church. As you live out your life in real time among real people in real life, people catch on to what you envision for the church's future. Start investing in people and others will catch on to what you're doing and will want to join you in making a difference in the church.

2. Unpack your personal baggage.

Each pastor is human and carries personal issues (baggage) into ministry from past experiences, particularly their family of origin. If you haven't faced your personal demons, being a solo pastor will force them to emerge in ways that may destroy ministry credibility. You can do all the right ministry actions, but personal grief and loss from deep wounds will surface, creating tensions. It's difficult to get your own life together while you're immersed in pastoring a church. One way, if needed, is to find a counselor who can help you process your feelings, hurts, and pains. Sometimes

> *No church is too small, community too broken, or people too ill-equipped to begin the work of evangelism.*
>
> —*Ed Stetzer*

just talking deeply with a good friend or mentor is enough, but the earlier you do this in your life, the less likely your untapped feelings will damage your ministry.

3. Lead from the floor as well as the stage.

Leadership in a solo-pastor church takes place among the people rather than out in front of them. While it's true that leaders have followers, this doesn't translate into always being in the front. If you ask people to trust you from a distance, they will to an extent. But allowing people greater access to you results in greater authority, if you're genuine. True leadership emerges from the midst of the people in solo-pastor churches. You can and should, of course, lead from the pulpit. Yet leadership power from the pulpit is supported by the trust engendered from ministry among the people. Nehemiah is an example of leading from the pack. When threatened, he was advised to stay out of danger, away from his enemies. Instead, he recognized that his place was among the people working near their homes on the wall, where arrows could harm and fighting could break out at any time. When you stand with the people—supporting them and experiencing the same challenges—they will follow.

4. Realize that you have influence, not power.

During the beginning of your solo-pastor ministry, you have only a small amount of authority and power, but you will have influence. Use what little authority and power you have sparingly. You're only a leader if you have followers. To be fruitful you'll need to get others to buy into your sense of mission and vision. It takes courage to actually lead people. Some solo pastors are no more than politicians who make promises but don't deliver. To lead, one must take courageous action. The major decision is to decide to be a leader and begin to use whatever amount of influence or power you possess. People will respect you for your character, not your political power. Recall how Jesus had authority even though he held no office, and how he turned down the prestige others wished to give him. His authority came from his words and his life, and so will yours.

5. *Lead the people, not the organization.*

As a solo pastor you'll be tempted to focus on changing the organizational structure of the church, but that's not leadership. God doesn't call you to exert leadership *on* people but to *lead* people. That's an entirely different calling. Remember, you're leading people, not an organization.

Resist the urge to focus on changing the constitution, bylaws, or church structure until you know the people well. The reality is any organizational structure can work well if the people are unified in their passion and direction. One of the marks of the early church was its unity of "one heart and soul" (Acts 4:32). Seek to create a oneness of heart, soul, and mind before changing the structure.

As a solo pastor, you'll discover that most churches are structured to keep you from leading. Your church may have a system of boards, committees, and policies that bind your hands rather than release you to lead. Some churches have boards that see their purpose as keeping the pastor under control rather than allowing them to lead. Such a church tries to limit leadership rather than maximize it. Romans 12:6–8 indicates that gifts, like leadership, are to be celebrated, not limited. But it's best to work with your church's structure, not against it, at least in the beginning of your ministry.

6. *Focus on the basics of ministry.*

The basics are the basics for a reason—they're basic. The basics for church ministry are evangelism, assimilation, and education. Another way to put this is finding people, keeping people, and developing people. In order for any church to be effective for the long haul, it needs to keep finding *new* people, assimilating *new* people, and training *new* people. New people must be added to the mix. What solo pastors often find is that no new people have been added to the church for years. This automatically stunts a

> *A pastor's influence is driven more by their internal character than by their ability to carry out programs.*

church's growth. Without new people, a church gets too comfortable. New challenges, ideas, and perspectives are not discovered. Whatever solo pastors do, they must help the church reach new people for Christ (find them), connect the new people to the church (keep them), and develop the new people (train them). This is done best through modeling. Rest assured that no one in the church is likely to share the gospel more than you. If you expect the people to speak to others about the riches of faith in Christ, they must see you doing so.

7. Build a team.

You will need to build a team who can help fulfill the vision of the church. Now, a lack of finances may keep you from hiring staff, but look around and find some people who can give you, say, three to five hours of time a week. Challenge them to be on your staff. Then work with those who respond to form a team. If you want your church to grow, you'll need more leaders. Generally, a church will grow at a rate of ten people for every leader in the church. A leader by definition has followers. So, in a solo-pastor church of one hundred people, you'll typically have ten leaders. The breakdown often looks like this: one pastor, two board members, and seven teachers or ministry leaders (of men, women, children, etc.). Find someone who shows evidence of being a leader and spend time with them. Invest in them. If you look for leaders, you'll find them.

Giving up control is hard. In a solo-pastor church, you will automatically end up doing many types of ministry. Over time you may start to think you're the only one who can do ministry well. That's a trap for sure. If you want your church to thrive, you must learn to consciously and constantly give up ministry to others. Yes, some people will not do as well as you could, but others will do better than you. Unless you give up control, the church will never advance any further than your ability to control it, which isn't very far.

8. Pivot when necessary.

You must be able to pivot as the church grows larger. One reason churches stay small is that solo pastors don't make the transition to leading in a new way that allows churches to grow. Your leadership by example never changes, but the way you engage the church does. Think of it this way. In a smaller church you engage people one-on-one, but as a church grows larger, you engage them through groups. In a smaller church you'll connect with others as their personal caregiver, while in a midsize church you'll connect more as the church's director of ministry programs. When the church becomes larger, you'll engage the people as the leader by casting vision and setting direction. Up to about one hundred worshipers, leading as a solo pastor works, but as the church makes the transition from one hundred to about two hundred people, you need to start adding additional pastors. If you've already started building a team with the people in the church, it's a natural progression to hire your first staff members. Many solo pastors are unprepared for the way their role changes as the church grows. Solo pastors often see a church grow to about 125 people using their people-oriented soft skills (e.g., visitation, care, counseling), but the church's growth bogs down thereafter because they don't or can't pivot to using more leader-oriented hard skills (e.g., vision casting, goal setting, long-range planning).

LEADING AS A SOLO PASTOR begins with relating to the people and church structure as they are rather than as you wish they were. Be the leader the church needs now, not what it will need in some mythical future. Then take it to where God wants it to be. This happens by building solid relationships, which is the focus of the next chapter.

THREE QUESTIONS

1. What frustrations have you experienced as a solo pastor when trying to create a vision for the future? Do you relate to the opening conversation? If so, in what way?
2. Which of the basics of leading described in this chapter do you see in your own ministry? What do you do well and not so well?
3. Since people buy into your vision when they buy into you, how are you helping people in your own church buy into you?

TWO IDEAS

1. Write down a list of the personal baggage (issues or struggles) you have brought into ministry. How does it keep you from being effective? How can you begin to unpack this baggage so you travel lighter in ministry?
2. Think through and develop a theology of leadership. What do you believe is the proper way to lead your church? How does it fit with the reality of your current situation? With your actual practice of leading? What needs to change for you to be a more effective leader?

PART 2

The Solo Pastor
Meets the People

FOUR

Build Relationships

With every action, you are doing two things: building trust or mistrust.

—Mark H. Senter III

H i, guys," the waitress greeted Jim and Bill as they walked into the diner for their monthly breakfast confab.

"Good morning," Jim replied, sitting down at the table, while Bill mumbled a similar greeting.

After giving their normal order and catching up on small talk, Jim asked, "So, what would you like to talk about today?"

"I've been thinking a lot about our last few conversations. One thing you said last month has been on my mind quite a bit since then."

"What's that?" Jim inquired.

"You mentioned that people only buy into your vision when they buy into you."

"That's right."

"Well, I'd like to unpack that a bit more this week."

"Okay," Jim began. "Think of it this way. Leadership is all about trust. If people are going to follow your vision for their church, they must be able to trust you. Unfortunately, in many solo-pastor churches, people have learned not to trust their pastors."

"How so?" Bill looked puzzled as he asked.

"It happens in a number of different ways. For example, the average solo pastor usually stays in a church less than four or five years. It's likely that pastors before you challenged the church to a big vision—say, a building program—which the people accepted. Then, after the big vision got going, the pastor left. The people felt abandoned. They were left with the long-term consequences of paying for the vision that the previous pastor had started but failed to finish. Once people have experienced this type of relationship a few times, they become wary of getting on board with the next pastor's vision."

"I totally get that," Bill acknowledged. "But I'm committed to staying in this church."

"You may be," Jim agreed, "but the people don't know if they can trust you to stay or not. It's not your fault. They're reacting to what they've experienced in the past."

Jim waited a moment for the waitress to fill up their coffee cups and then continued. "Let me give you another example of how trust is destroyed in the solo-pastor church. Unfortunately, in quite a number of situations, a church has a history of some trauma— say, a church split, a pastor's indiscretion, or a layperson's mishandling of church money. Such situations cause a major amount of spiritual and emotional hurt among the people. Many times people leave, but in almost every case the leaders of the church put measures in place to protect themselves from further hurt."

"How do they do that?" Bill said with interest.

"Essentially, the key family or leadership board consolidates their hold on the leadership power. The board may set new policies that require the entire church to vote on all new programs. Or the controlling family may refuse to support any new ventures proposed by the new pastor. Since the family comprises such a power block in the church, the new pastor can't do much of anything without them. So their lack of support effectively kills any new ideas. Or the entire church family may be so traumatized from past experience that they simply refuse to buy into the vision of a new pastor."

"Wow! I've never considered this before. I think that's part of the issue at my church. About a decade ago, the church was averaging close to two hundred in worship attendance, but they went through two jarring splits."

"That'll do it," Jim consented. "In order to protect themselves from future hurt, your people are reluctant to support your ideas."

"I can see how that happened. So, what can I do?" Bill questioned.

"It's all about relationships," Jim explained. "Leadership is built on a foundation of trust. It's difficult in a situation like yours, but the next step—and it's a long journey—is to build trust between yourself and your people. Trust needs to form and harden like glue before they'll buy into your vision. Remember: Christian ministry is never impersonal; it's always personal."

"How do I go about building trust?" Bill asked.

THIS CONVERSATION REVEALS one of the reasons solo pastors fail to gain support for ideas and plans: insufficient trust. Relationships predominate in solo-pastor churches. It is within relationships that trust is established, tried, and confirmed. The pastor's commitment to the people—the church—defines character and determines future effectiveness.

Loving relationships are foundational to focused, faithful, and fruitful ministry. Speaking to his early disciples, Jesus told them, "Follow Me, and I will make you fishers of men" (Matt. 4:19). "Follow Me" defines the relationship, while "make you fishers of men" defines the mission. Relationship comes before mission in the life of a church. The primary relationship is with God the Father through Jesus Christ his Son. However, the importance of relationships with both Christ and other people is seen throughout the early church. The disciples committed themselves to "the apostles' teaching and to fellowship, to the breaking of bread and to prayer" (Acts 2:42). They were of "one heart and soul," sharing their earthly goods with each other as needs arose (4:32). Paul also points out the crucial nature of relationships by calling attention to the reality that people follow leaders as they follow Christ. "Be imitators of me," Paul commands, "just as I also am of Christ" (1 Cor. 11:1; see also 1 Cor. 4:16; Phil. 3:17).

Regrettably, pastors struggle to create meaningful relationships with people, and trust is consequently undermined. Solo pastors may have good ideas, but the ideas will never be accepted unless the trust factor is in place. The trouble is that pastors think organizationally about the church before thinking relationally. A good rule to remember is this: whenever you hit resistance, strengthen the relationship before bringing in reinforcements.

Here are some insights and tips that Bill might find useful, and perhaps you will, too, as you seek to build trust with your people. Remember that with every action, you are doing one of two things: establishing trust or establishing mistrust.

1. People don't care how much you know until they know how much you care.

It's commonplace to hear this truism repeated, but it's especially true in the single-staff church. Solo pastors must find ways to say, "I care." One of the main ways to prove you care is through conversation. Entering into conversation is difficult due to a number of factors. Social media and electronic gadgetry pull all of us away from meaningful conversation. We also like to talk about ourselves and are pretty lousy at asking good questions. If you come across to your people as if you're selling them a vision like you would sell a product, you won't get far. Hence, you may find it helpful to track and examine the relational encounters you have with people in your church. How many lunches do you have with people each week? What do you talk about? What do you learn about the people? If we honestly care about people, we'll ask good questions: "Oh, you have a son? Tell me about him." "So, you like working with your hands? What do you like doing the most?" "It's nice to know you travel a lot. Where was your favorite destination?" If you can initiate good conversations, you'll build a foundation on which trust can develop.

2. Follow the social mores.

Social mores are the normal way of doing life in a particular place. They are the customary or acceptable ways to behave, and they affect actions, attire, and activities. To establish, build, and maintain credibility, it's essential that a solo pastor follow the basic social manners and customs of their setting. When Pastor Randy threw that cookie while at the dinner table, he violated a social norm even though he was being himself. Such actions destroy trust. To learn the basic social graces of your location, visit people at their workplaces, help out with chores around their homes, and work side by side with them on projects at church. Observe their behavior, but most of all ask for advice. What is the expected attire for Sunday morning or at a funeral or when visiting people in the hospital? While you may think some of the customs are silly, it's best to follow them until you gain enough trust to challenge them. At any rate, intentionally violating social mores will not help you build trust. So practice basic courtesy. If you've obviously violated someone's social mores, apologize for your behavior to get the relationship back on track.

3. Close the loop.

Most people desire to have friends. However, if you're a solo pastor, it's more important to be respected than liked. You should certainly strive to make friends with people in the church, but earn respect by doing what you say you'll do. One way to do so is to close the loop in relationships. Most of us have experienced a time when someone made a promise and then failed to follow through. The person didn't "close the loop."

Failing to return phone calls or answer emails is a regular occurrence but a poor communication skill. If you habitually stall on replying to others, you are undermining trust in your leadership. That doesn't mean you have to answer every call and email immediately, but you should respond in some way. You could say something like, "May I call you back in an hour?" Or, "I can't talk right now. When would be a good time to call you back?" For emails, simply reply, "I'm tied up right now, but I'll get back to you later today." Then make it your goal to close the loop by returning calls and replying to emails. Did you promise to get back to someone but haven't done so? Following up is a crucial communication skill, so be sure to close the loop with others.

4. Take your time.

Build credibility incrementally and patiently. Don't appear to be in a hurry. Time and taking time are essential for connection and relationship building. In the first couple years of your ministry, people are checking you out to see if you're trustworthy. They need to know from experience they can trust you with their hearts—their deep feelings, hurts, and pains. This comes only after they've seen you up close and personal in real ministry situations. So in the first couple years of ministry, remember to give people time. They will come around to support you fully in time.

As you build relationships, gauge your time wisely. Don't over-schedule. Make room for interruptions. For example, a knock

> *Wisdom is the reward you get for a lifetime of listening when you'd have preferred to talk.*
>
> *—Doug Larson*

on your office door may reveal a member asking, "Hey, pastor, do you have time for coffee?" Yes, you do. Take the time. These are not interruptions; they are God-ordained times for building relationships.

5. Give yourself time too.

Related to taking time is the reality that solo pastors are often young and inexperienced. Even if a pastor had an internship, they're normally not ready to be the resident spiritual leader in a church. Unfortunately, seminary students graduate thinking they are completely trained and adequate to lead a church. Leading a church can't be learned in a seminary or other educational setting. It takes a certain spiritual depth to lead a church well. There's a reason most countries of the world require their president or premier to be a certain age before taking office—it takes time to build maturity. Pastoral maturity comes from starting, trying, making mistakes, and learning from them. One sign of a spiritually mature church is the congregation's ability to be forgiving of its pastor, nurturing them and helping them learn.

6. Ask others for advice.

If you go about the work of pastoring as though you don't need others, you are indicating that you don't value others in the work. Asking for advice shows that you respect others' gifts, knowledge, feelings, and experience. A successful solo pastor always asks for help. In the early days of your ministry, have a beginner's mindset. If you approach people as the expert, you will look for confirmation of your own viewpoint and will learn nothing. It's more profitable to approach a new ministry as a beginner, looking for that one tidbit of information to help you understand the church. It's only as you enter into conversations with a beginner's mindset that you'll build trust.

It's a mistake, of course, to contact people only when you need something. Have you ever had a friend you heard from only when they needed something? It was annoying, right? If you contact people in the church only when you need something, you'll run the risk of making people feel used. So be sure to meet with people just for the relationship. Ask for nothing; just touch base. Then when you do need advice, it'll be given in a context of trust and respect.

7. Connect on an emotional level.

This takes asking people a lot of questions and listening to what they say. Use words and phrases like "Why?" "I think there's a story behind that," and "Tell me more." Such responses show that you care for them and are willing to listen to what they think before recommending changes or giving advice. Be sure to take notes as you listen, for doing so conveys your care.

Try to keep your own emotions under control as you listen, really listen, to what others say. To listen better, try these ideas. First, summarize what the person said before you make your reply. Second, repeat the last three words of the person's comment before you launch into your response. Third, ask two questions about their comment before you respond.

Consider whether the person is expressing a valid issue or merely revealing a personal problem. Say things like "I hear what you're saying" or "I don't understand, so tell me more." You don't always need to have an immediate answer or the last word. Feel comfortable saying, "I'm not sure, but I'll find out" or "I need to think about that for a while." Then get back to them in a reasonable amount of time with your thoughts.

8. Take responsibility.

The primary way of gaining trust is to do your job well. While relationships are foundational, if you're doing your job well, others will tend to trust you. Thus, if you want others to cooperate, you must show yourself responsible. One pastor recommends developing responsibility by "being warm, open, and encouraging; being an example of responsibility; and giving those you lead opportunities to practice responsibility." Taking responsibility means, of course, following up on your promises and keeping your word. It also implies telling the truth. Thus, refrain from telling lies. Big ones will damage others' trust in you, but so will small ones. It's tempting to tell small lies to keep from hurting someone's feelings or to slant an answer to your own gain. If you find yourself shading an answer one way for one person and then another way for a different person, you're playing with the truth. Or if you find yourself changing or withholding facts to sway people to your viewpoint, you're manipulating the truth. One would hope that pastors don't practice such deceptions, but people in solo-pastor churches have seen it before. As a solo pastor, you'll have to prove yourself trustworthy before people will buy into your vision.

9. *Love people; learn history.*

A solo pastor is a historian—they get to know the people in the church and understand what has taken place throughout the years. And they should do this before making changes. It's long been noted that when new pastors arrive, they attempt to make changes, often to the constitution and bylaws of the church. Doing so says to the people that the pastor is the expert and the people don't know much of anything. This attitude and approach undermine trust. They communicate not only distrust but even rejection of the people. So try the following: (1) Build a relational map. As you start getting to know people, make a map of relationships. Who knows whom? Who respects whom? What are the family and friendship connections? What are each person's skills, abilities, talents, and gifts? What do they value and care about? Then work with these relational connections in mind. (2) Discover how the Holy Spirit is working in the church. Where is Christ present already in the community? The history of the church, particularly that of the last five to ten years, will give you insight. What programs or ministries are honored? Where has the church shown growth? How have newcomers connected with the church? A congregation may not be doing things the way you were taught, but something is happening. Find it and build on it.

10. Build trust in God.

Solo-pastor churches must build their trust in God. Fruitful ministry requires faith, but it's sometimes difficult for the solo-pastor church to take reasonable risks for fear of failure. If you are a solo pastor, your ministry effectiveness is established by how well you help people trust God. Here are some ways to start. (1) Focus on your hope in Christ. Help the people recognize and believe that God will provide the resources needed to fulfill the ministry he desires from them. (2) Stress the importance of asking "What does God want us to accomplish?" rather than "How can we keep the ministry alive?" (3) Emphasize the positive over the negative. In bad situations, it's easy to be negative. Effective solo pastors learn to emphasize the positive over the negative. Rather than dwelling on the difficulties of a situation, find the positive and emphasize it. (4) Trust people to do ministry. Release people to use their own gifts and talents in ministry. Stress the fact that God gives the ministry to the people and that you're there to equip them to do the work. (5) Encourage people to trust each other. Note the importance of seeing how God works through others. As you practice these ideas, you'll observe people growing in their trust of God too.

11. Listen—really listen.

Have you ever caught yourself zoning out while listening to another person? Most people listen enough to formulate what they are going to say in reply, not to hear what the other person is really saying. This tactic undermines trust and credibility because you end up putting words in other people's mouths that they didn't actually say. Or you answer questions that people didn't actually ask. Either way, poor listening skills result in poor communication, lost opportunities, and unnecessary mistakes. Worse, people get the message you can't be trusted to understand them.

When you listen, people begin to believe in you. When they believe in you, they'll follow you. Start by talking with as many people as possible: parents, children, older saints, long-term members, and recent newcomers. Ask questions such as "What is this church all about?" "Why are you here?" "What is working well?" "What is not working so well?" "If you'd like for me to do one thing in the next few years, what would it be?" Don't promise anything at this point, but listen. Listening builds relationships and trust. Listening allows patterns to develop. God often speaks through his saints—their joys, pains, and dreams.

12. Create a culture of honor and respect.

Never talk down to people. People may not have the technical skills you have developed in school, but they usually have some level of Christian maturity, having walked with Christ for a number of years. Don't correct them in a heavy manner or show off your Greek or Hebrew vocabulary. Say what you mean, and learn how to say it best. Speak up and be honest, but do so with graciousness. Never gossip or criticize anyone, as you never know who will quote you and whom they will tell what you said.

Lift others up, and praise pastors from previous years when possible. Honor the longtime members, workers, and families. Be careful about criticizing other pastors' churches or ministries, even if you're certain you are correct and they are not. Criticism doesn't raise your credibility and trust level in the eyes of your own people, while a bit of humility does.

13. Stay above reproach.

First Timothy 3:2 reminds us that pastors are to be above reproach. In one way or another, all the suggestions previously listed are connected to staying above reproach. In an age when our smallest communication is often broadcast for the world to hear, solo pastors must take time to think through how staying above reproach affects their trustworthiness. This is particularly relevant in regard to the use of email and social media. The internet is an open book. What you post or send may be passed on, misunderstood, and misinterpreted. Our world is very suspicious, and people will use your seemingly harmless posts and email communication to affirm their suspicions. As a solo pastor, you must guard your communication. One pastor suggests asking the following questions before you push the Send button:

- Have I written anything that might harm someone else?
- Does this post represent Jesus well?
- Is it possible this communication could be misunderstood, misinterpreted, or misrepresented?
- Would I be ashamed if this content or these photos were shared with my congregation?
- Is my email or post the result of my personal frustration, and is it self-serving?

Asking these questions and answering them honestly may point out the need to hit the Delete button rather than the Send button.

EXPLAIN TO PEOPLE that you're not there to run the church but to get to know them and improve the good work they are already doing. Find resources to fix problems they point out. Celebrate all victories and improvements, no matter how small or insignificant. Be careful, however, not to play the game of pastor fetch. More about that in the next chapter.

THREE QUESTIONS

1. Do you contact others only when you need them to do something for the church?
2. Is there anyone you need to get back to in person, by phone, or by email?

3. Have you had a conversation lately and you can't recall what the other person said?

TWO IDEAS

1. Work hard this week at really listening to what others are saying to you. Keep a small notebook with brief sentences about your conversations. Doing this will help you maintain focus and gain a better understanding of what others communicate.

2. Before you reply to people this week, state back to them what they said. Practice repeating the last three words they said as an aid to focusing on your conversations.

FIVE

Stop Playing Fetch

God loves you . . . and everyone else has a wonderful plan for your life.

—Unknown

M y wife and I had just started dozing off," Bill shared, "when my cell phone rang. As you know, when someone calls that late, it's usually not good."

"Yep, I understand." Jim smiled. "I've had quite a few late-night calls myself."

"I'll bet you have," Bill continued. "So, I prepared myself for the worst, but this particular call stunned me. Sylvia, a longtime member of my church and the leader of our women's group, was the caller. She said, 'Pastor, I was driving by the church just a few minutes ago and saw that the light is on in the women's restroom. Would you please go over to the church and turn it off? You know, we need to save on the electric bill.'"

"Uh-huh," Jim mumbled. "What did you say?"

"Now, I'm normally willing to respond to reasonable requests, but this seemed beyond reasonable. My first thought was to ask why she didn't just stop, go into the church, and turn the light off herself. She has a key. Fortunately, I suppressed that thought and told her I'd take care of it. After the call was over, I went back to bed and fell asleep. The next morning I turned the light off after I got to my office."

"Well, I've had similar conversations with some of my people," added Jim. "Right after I came to Grace Church, a deacon called and asked if I'd be sure to get over to the church an hour early and turn on the heat. Like you, I wondered why he didn't just go to church early and turn on the heat himself."

"Sounds like you've been where I'm at," Bill noted.

"True, and that reminds me of a church I visited a few years ago. The pastor asked me to meet him at church and then go to lunch to talk about ministry. As we started to leave the church, the pastor went around and turned off all the lights before we left. I thought to myself, *Now that's what you hire a pastor to do—turn off the lights.*"

"Oh my!" Bill sighed. "I bet someone asked him to do it to save electricity. People at my church make these types of requests all the time. For example, after I'd been at the church just three weeks, an elder asked me to drop by the office supply store and pick up some boxes of materials he'd ordered for the church office. Of course, being new, I did as he asked, but I wondered who had been his gofer before I arrived—maybe it was the previous pastor."

JIM AND BILL'S CONVERSATION illustrates a game that some people play with their solo pastor: pastor fetch. The concept comes from a game people play with their dog. Have you ever seen a person throw a ball and then send their dog to fetch it? Each time the dog returns the ball to their owner, they're rewarded with the words "Good dog." Each time a pastor does what people in their church ask, they're rewarded with the words "Good pastor." Turn off the lights. "Good pastor." Pick up the mail. "Good pastor." Turn on the heat. "Good pastor." Heaven forbid the pastor doesn't do what they're asked. "Bad pastor!"

If you're a solo pastor, you no doubt have played this game, perhaps often. After a while, it gets tiresome. You just want to drop the ball, lie down, and stop playing the game. Playing fetch with a pastor is a common game among church members in solo-pastor churches for a number of reasons.

1. Solo pastors tend to come and go.

It's not uncommon for solo-pastor churches to have three pastors in a seven-year span. One older study found that the average tenure for all pastors is 4.9 years overall, while the average of the shortest tenures is only 2.2 years.[1] More recent studies indicate the length of pastorates is increasing, with some reporting a median of six years instead of four. While precise statistics vary from denomination to denomination, it's safe to say that average tenure in a local church is between five to seven years; however, the average tenure of solo pastors is 28 percent shorter than pastors in multi-staff churches, which means they stay 3.6 to 5 years.[2] With such short tenures, it's impossible for pastors to establish a new culture of expectations, so they acquiesce to the expectations of the people. If a pastor tries to change the expectations, church members patiently wait for a pastor who doesn't do their bidding to leave.

2. Solo pastors are viewed as workers—the lowest level of workers at that!

The constant movement of pastors has led to a redefinition of the pastor's role in a local church. Rather than seeing the solo pastor as a shepherd who leads the flock, people view them as a hired hand who does their bidding. Long-term members expect their pastor to be what used to be called an errand boy, or a gofer. This title is for the person who works at the lowest level of an organization.

3. Solo pastors are often inexperienced.

New pastors are thankful just to have the opportunity to preach and teach. Thus, they submit to whatever the people expect in an effort to keep their job or because they honestly don't know their proper role. Since they are inexperienced, they naturally allow more experienced church leaders to establish the leadership culture. If the culture expects the solo pastor to have a wide-open door and do whatever is requested, they fall into the trap of playing pastor fetch. This pulls the pastor away from the ministry priorities that might help the church grow.

4. Solo pastors often don't know their role.

What are the proper expectations for a solo pastor? Before a solo pastor accepts a call or appointment to a church, they and the potential congregation normally have surface-level conversations about expectations. Ephesians 4:11–12 points to the key role of all pastors: equipping the saints for the work of ministry. Doing so requires a servant's heart, as implied in the word *equipping*. The word refers to the act of a doctor setting a bone or a fisherman mending nets, each of which is hands-on work—that is, work of service to another person. What the passage doesn't impose on pastors is the requirement to chase every ball of expectation tossed by well-meaning church members.

5. Solo pastors often misunderstand the call to servanthood.

Solo pastors rationalize their willingness to play pastor fetch by recalling the need to be a servant. Solo pastors are servants, but they are servants of God more than servants of the people. Godly leaders throughout the biblical record are referred to as God's servants:

Abraham (Gen. 26:24)
Moses (Exod. 14:31)
Caleb (Num. 14:24)

Samuel (1 Sam. 3:9)

David (1 Chron. 17:4)

Elijah (2 Kings 9:36)

Isaiah (Isa. 20:3)

Jesus told his followers, "You know that the rulers of the Gentiles lord it over them, and their great men exercise authority over them. It is not this way among you, but whoever wishes to become great among you shall be your servant, and whoever wishes to be first among you shall be your slave; just as the Son of Man did not come to be served, but to serve, and to give His life a ransom for many" (Matt. 20:25–28; see also Matt. 23:1–12; Luke 22:26). Pastors are primarily God's servants who humbly serve the flock of God. Certainly, pastors must have an attitude of servanthood, but this does not mean pastors are to play games like fetch.

6. *Solo pastors are faced with increasing diversity in today's congregations.*

Diversity, of course, comes in many forms—ethnicity, age, income, education, and so on—and increasing diversity of any kind brings multiple challenges. One challenge is the increasing number of expectations placed on pastors. While a pastor used to have a standard set of expectations—visit people, preach, marry people, bury people—today there are as many expectations as there are

Churchgoers often think of the pastor as performing a service for them. They are as demanding and particular as if they had bought a suit from a clothing store and didn't like the cuff length.

—*Ben Patterson*

70

people. Each member expects the pastor to meet their individual needs and desires. Instead of one set of expectations in a church of, say, one hundred worshipers, there are now more likely one hundred different expectations. Some want a pastoral visit; others never want to see the pastor at their home. Some expect a hospital call; others don't want the pastor to see them when they're ill. The list goes on and on, making it impossible for the solo pastor to please everyone. But that doesn't stop them from trying.

7. Solo pastors are often compared to previous pastors.

The only example many laypersons have is a pastor who does it all. One solo pastor served his church for twenty years. By all accounts, he was a loving pastor who provided excellent care for his people. Unfortunately, personal wounds from a past church caused him to do it all. In worship services he played the piano, gave announcements, prayed for the offering, and preached the sermon—he did everything. During the week he picked up the mail, answered the phone, and generally made himself available for every game of pastor fetch the people desired to play. For twenty years that's the only example the congregation had of a pastor's role. You can imagine the challenge the next pastor faced in changing the expectations of what the pastor should do. For many people raised in solo-pastor churches, the pastor was the go-to person for every program, issue, or service the church offered.

8. Solo pastors don't delegate.

It's rare to hear stories of solo pastors who are good delegators of ministry work. While solo pastors preach about the importance of every person using their spiritual gifts for the work of ministry, the reality is few are able to make this work in practice. Yet as long as there is at least one other person in your church, you can focus on delegation. It's a philosophy of ministry before it's a practice.

Take stock of the people in your church. Who's there? What spiritual gifts do they have to be tapped? Ask people, "What do you think our church is good at doing? Who are the gifted people in our church? What should we do in the next few years?" Listen until you begin to hear the same ideas and people mentioned over and over again. This activity gives you insight into the strengths and needs of the church as well as who the gifted people are. By getting to know the people, you'll put pieces together for future ministry. Then determine not to do anything unless someone suggests it and volunteers to do it. You can guide them, but let them decide what to do and then let them do it.

One more word about delegation. One of the most important things to learn as a solo pastor is to delegate to God. It is a fact of life that there are a number of things you can do nothing about. Don't let people put all their problems on your shoulders. Something is your problem only when you can do something about it. We need to help carry others' burdens (Gal. 6:2), but it's also necessary for others to carry their own loads (v. 5). When you encounter requests that are not yours to bear, give them to God in prayer. Communicate to your people that God is your leader and there are things only he can do.

9. Solo pastors enjoy being the center of the work.

The reasons solo pastors enjoy being at the center of the work vary from an emotional need for security to a strong call to ministry to the fun of being in the action. Some solo pastors take on too much because there are so many exciting things to do: preaching, teaching, caring, loving, supporting, and so on. Other pastors find a measure of satisfaction in being needed in almost every situation. They desire for others to be dependent on them; they want to be needed more than they desire to make disciples. Feelings of importance and authority also come from being at the center of church life. Again, the reasons are many, but the result is the same: pastors end up playing pastor fetch.

10. Solo pastors don't know how to lead themselves.

Once you've decided what your job is, you can concentrate on some practical ways to work with your people. Here's one way

> *I did a lot of fetching, but I never learned to sit.*
> *Eventually I learned to stop asking, "How can I*
> *perform better?" and to start asking, "How can*
> *I fit into what God is doing?"*
>
> —*Eugene Peterson*

to start. Use a calendar as an appointment book. You can do this on your phone, on a computer, or with a standard paper planner. Divide up the week into twenty-one sections: morning, afternoon, and evening for all seven days. Using broad categories like this will allow you to set priorities for each section while giving you enough open time to handle the inevitable interruptions that happen in a solo-pastor church. Next, schedule certain blocks of time for sermon preparation, visitation, and so on.

Watch your schedule for a few weeks. Determine what a typical day is like for you. If you schedule church work for eighteen or more segments, it's too much. Note how many interruptions you get, such as phone calls, people who drop by, and so on. Once you have a typical day and week in view, share it with your church leaders. Tell them, "I want to share with you about a day in the life of your pastor. Here's what I'm doing. This is what I've done for the past two weeks."

Establish a mental scale to determine what is urgent and what is not urgent. For example, a visit to the hospital may be urgent; a trip to the church to turn off a light is most likely not. When people ask you to run an errand, make a call, or care for a problem, weigh the request on your mental scale. If it's not urgent, ask them to do it for you. Start replying with sentences like "I appreciate your concern. Would it be possible for you to take care of this for me?" "That seems to be an interest of yours. Might you be able to take charge of it?" "I sense you care about this a great deal, so I'm going to appoint you to do it each week." The best person to do the job is the person who notices the need. If you keep an I-will-do-it-all attitude, what you're really saying is "I don't believe in using other people's gifts." If you really believe in community and that others should serve, you have to give the ball back to them. You have to learn to rely on others, to trust them with the work of ministry.

To a great extent, availability goes with the role of solo pastor. You can, however, slow down the game of pastor fetch by setting boundaries: (1) Tell your board and congregation what your standard schedule is and when you'd like to be left alone for study. Many will seek to honor your request, which will reduce the number of unscheduled calls and drop-in visits. (2) Learn the fine art of saying no. Your congregation may expect you to have an open-door policy and be ready and able to answer every request. If you have a secretary, even a part-time one, instruct them to guard your study time by taking a message for you and telling visitors you're working on your sermon and can't be disturbed. Be sure to put a message on your cell phone: "This is Pastor Gary. I'm unable to take your call right now as I have another commitment. I'll be through at [choose a specific time] and will be happy to call you back between [a set time]. If this is an emergency, please call [give the name and number of a person who can contact you in case of emergency]." (3) When people surprise you in the hallway or elsewhere and ask for an appointment, tell them to call you the next day to set up a time. Resist making appointments when first engaged. It's easy to say yes to things in the hurry of Sunday morning—commitments you'll regret later on. Do this even if you have your schedule on your phone. Give yourself space to look at your appointment book before committing to a specific time and place to meet. (4) When people drop by your office, stand up and meet them at the door. Determine if the interruption is important. If it isn't, talk standing up; if it is, ask them to sit down. Remember, though, if they sit down, it's going to be a l-o-n-g interruption. Another option is to ask to meet them at their office, their home, or a restaurant. Meeting at these places allows you to leave more easily.

The point is, if people perceive you as highly interruptible, they'll interrupt you. If they think you'll do everything they ask, they'll ask you. If they detect you'll answer every call, they'll call you. In truth, you don't have to be available to everyone all the time. That's poor leadership. Good leadership is letting people know *when* you are available. By managing people's expectations, you'll reduce the number of people trying to play pastor fetch. You don't let people spend your money, so why do you let them spend your time? You must constantly remind people of your commitment to the most important priorities.

A CHURCH IS THE MOST COMPLEX organization to lead. It's what management experts call "goal-conflicted." One goal is to care for people; another is to send people out in ministry. The church is made up of the walking wounded—people in need of healing or those who have recovered just enough to serve. There's a continuing dynamic of balancing relationships of love and care with challenging people to witness and serve. The number of possible relationships in a church of 100 people is 4,950. With so many potential connections, a solo pastor can't continue to play the game of pastor fetch.

So take a day to go somewhere alone where you can spend time thinking. Bring yourself into God's presence in prayer, and then think about the kind of ministry you'd like to have in five years. Picture a day or a week in your life. What would you like to see yourself doing on a typical day or in a typical week? This process will clarify what you really want to do in ministry.

THREE QUESTIONS

1. How do you separate reasonable from unreasonable requests? Describe your process or thinking in doing so.
2. In what ways have you played pastor fetch in the past? Share one or two examples.
3. Do you find it easy or difficult to say no to unreasonable requests? Why?

TWO IDEAS

1. Make a list of all the things you do each week. Then sit back and look at the list and ask yourself, "How do I feel about this list? Am I doing the right things? Am I spending the right amount of time on each item? What should I not be doing?" Share the ten most important things you do each week with a few trusted colleagues and ask them, "How do you feel about what I'm doing?" You might hear some different perspectives. Also consider asking your spouse, your board, and some friends to make their own lists of what they think you should be doing as the pastor. A comparison of their lists with yours may surprise you. Note the things you need to let go, and seek out other people to do them. Keep giving away work to others until each of these tasks has been reassigned.
2. Take some time to review your ministry (job?) description. What expectations, requirements, or tasks does it place on you? How do they align with your gifts, talents, or abilities? Consider revising it so it fits your skills accurately. Then discuss it with your board.

SIX

Check Bullies

Pastors are revered one day, reviled the next.

—Anonymous

Sorry I couldn't meet for breakfast this week," Bill began, "but I had one of those emergency calls from a church leader. He wanted to meet for breakfast, and I felt it was something I needed to do."

"It's no problem," assured Jim. "Trust me. I've had similar requests over the years. How did the breakfast meeting go?"

"It went well, until he gave me an ultimatum."

Looking concerned, Jim asked, "What did he say?"

"He said, and I quote, 'Now I want you to know that I make the major decisions in our church. The last pastor always ran his sermon topics past me before preaching, and I expect you to do the same.'"

"Wow! That's pretty bold. So what did you do?"

"To put it bluntly, I was dumbfounded. I just murmured a few words to the effect that I'd prefer to select my own sermon topics and then didn't say much else. I just wanted to end the breakfast as quickly as possible."

"I'll bet. Times like that are very uncomfortable. One time a church bully cornered me after a worship service and declared, 'Pastor, you do the marrying, burying, evangelizing, praying, and counseling. That's what we pay you for, and we'll do the rest.' It really set me back on my heels."

"I've never had something like that happen before," Bill confessed. "What's the best way to handle a person or comment like that? Do you have any wisdom you can give me?"

PASTORING A CHURCH is not easy. It's certainly not for the fainthearted. If the solo pastor needs to be liked by everyone in the church, they will not be able to manage a church bully. Church bullies exist in churches, and solo pastors must often deal with them alone (although it's best to deal with them with other strong members in the church). They may be called other names, such as power brokers, controllers, hasslers, troublemakers, church bosses, or, a particular favorite, Clyde (as in col-lide!).

This conversation doesn't imply that all disagreements between people are evil or a type of bullying. There's room in the church for different points of view and gracious disagreements. Unfortunately, in some cases individuals or groups of people engage in acts that promote their personal agendas and desire for power. Bullying is best defined as repeated aggressive behavior intended to hurt another person or group of persons with the agenda of gaining power and control. Power exists in every church, but it's normally used with humility and grace. Bullying is a type of abusive power. When exercised in a church, it hurts not just the pastor but the entire congregation, as the people live in fear of the bully.

It's easy to point out the schoolyard bully, but church bullies are more sophisticated. They use tactics that sound spiritual and normally practice them in unseen lunches, board meetings, or one-on-one conversations. Their behavior is usually not observed by the majority of the congregation, which allows them to fly under the radar. Their behavior creates a toxic environment, at least for the solo pastor.

In most situations you can identify a bully by their desire to take over your job, or at least to tell you how to do your job. One pastor told the following story: "I was a new pastor just out of seminary. The church voted into office a lay Christian education director, and he scheduled a meeting with me the next week. The day we met, the first words out of his mouth were 'Now listen here. You work for *me*! The church voted *me* in as director of education, and I'm in charge.'" One can imagine that working with a church bully of this sort is painful.

Unfortunately, church bullies are common. It's difficult to know how to handle them, since everyone is expected to be nice at church. They're especially dangerous when they maneuver themselves into official positions—elder, deacon, trustee, financial chairperson, and so on. They don't need an official position to bully others, but they do need an enemy—that is, someone to fight. Quite often their enemy is the solo pastor.

The apostle John talks about one such bully. "I wrote something to the church; but Diotrephes, who loves to be first among them, does not accept what we say. For this reason, if I come, I will call attention to his deeds which he does, unjustly accusing us with wicked words; and not satisfied with this, he himself does not receive the brethren, either, and he forbids those who desire to do so and puts them out of the church. Beloved, do not imitate what is evil, but what is good" (3 John 9–11). John mentions five characteristics that indicate Diotrephes is a bully: (1) he loves self-exaltation and pride—"loves to be first among them" (v. 9); (2) he rejects counsel—"does not accept what we say" (v. 9); (3) he makes unjust accusations against leaders—"unjustly accusing us with wicked words" (v. 10); (4) he is not warm to other brothers and sisters in Christ—"he himself does not receive the brethren" (v. 10); and (5) he tries to dominate others—"forbids those who desire to do so and puts them out of the church" (v. 10).

As seen in Diotrephes, the underlying motives of church bullies are always power and control—that is, they want the power and control in the church. Bullies either already have or want to have some level of power and control over church ministries, decisions, or people. They tend to think of themselves as leaders who are willing to speak up when others won't. Thus, in their own minds, the church would be in major trouble if not for their courageous willingness to take charge. They come in many types and are revealed in numerous situations, yet their tactics are common. Here are a number of bullying tactics solo pastors face.

Spreading rumors. One type of church bully is the church tattletale. They are nosy and constantly monitor the pastor's activities. When in conversation with the pastor, the tattletale asks lots of probing questions. In time, such questioning seems like they are pumping the pastor to discover something they can use to undermine their ministry.

Getting angry. Some bullies yell, scream, throw tantrums, or otherwise show anger in an effort to intimidate or humiliate others. These outbursts happen unexpectedly at seemingly odd or unnecessary times.

Making false accusations. This is a primary tactic used by church bullies. They accuse others of making mistakes, comments, and statements they didn't make. And a chief one: they accuse others of being unbiblical. The accusations are used in an attempt to discredit or set up others for failure. Specific criticisms are usually based on something that is only partially true or factual, but the bully makes it sound like it is completely true.

Glaring or staring. Bullies try to intimidate others by glaring or staring intently at them. They may fold their arms, turn away in disgust, or roll their eyes at comments made by others. Such a show of hostility through body language serves to exert power or control over others.

Forging allies. Bullies like to gather supporters in an effort to feel more powerful. They may encourage people to join them in criticizing others or to turn against others in some manner. Deep inside they are insecure and sense their identity is under threat. Thus, they seek alliances to build up their own feelings of importance. When speaking, they love to infer that others are saying things in agreement with them.

Making dismissive comments. Attempting to embarrass others is another tactic of bullies. Making side comments such as "Oh, that's silly" and "Humph, no one believes that" serves as a way to show disrespect.

Using silence. Giving others the silent treatment to ostracize them is a common tactic of church bullies. Phone calls go unanswered, emails receive no reply, requests for meetings are unheeded. In meetings, direct questions are ignored or skipped over.

Disregarding success. Church bullies ignore or disregard excellent work by solo pastors, saying "It's not good enough." For the most part, the bully is not interested in results but mainly power and control. They may make up rules or recite expectations that put others in a bad light. During performance reviews, a bully may lie about the pastor's performance or even claim some credit for ministry success in an endeavor to shine the light away from the pastor.

Making demands. A bully may make ridiculous demands of the pastor, such as an impossible deadline or an unreasonable request, knowing that they can't be met. A solo pastor told the story of one church bully who demanded the pastor recite the books of the Bible in order. While the pastor had memorized the sixty-six books of the Bible as a child, he couldn't recall them in order under the pressure of the bully's demand. Outraged, the bully accused the pastor of being unfit for the pastoral position.

Retaliating. If a solo pastor tries to control, speak against, or report bullying behavior, the bully may react negatively. A bully may use insults, increased oversight, or some of the other tactics already noted.

Dealing with church bullies is uncomfortable at best, and dangerous to one's ministry at worst. Dealing with bullies is a complicated but necessary aspect of leading solo-pastor churches. Ignoring bullies leaves the church in serious danger. Be careful. When bullies use you for negative carping, complaining, grousing, and gossiping, this sort of behavior is agenda-driven.

Here are some insights and tips to guide you as a solo pastor to challenge and handle the bullies you may encounter.

1. If your church is a light on a hill, it will attract a few bugs.

Good churches attract a lot of people, and some of them will be odd or difficult or challenging—you name it. Expect them to come, and be ready to manage them. Start with prayer. It's powerful. God's Holy Spirit is at work in your church, so allow him time to work. Ask the Lord what to do. Listen to him speak through the Scriptures and other godly leaders. Other church members, particularly those who've been around awhile, know the problem. They've no doubt seen the bully work before. Talk with them. Listen to their concerns, insights, and suggestions.

2. Think of the bully as a rock in a stream.

A church is like a stream in which there are a lot of rocks—some bigger than others. As the stream moves along, some rocks will block it, causing it to pool up. If water can't move out of the pool, it will eventually stagnate. If a particular rock is blocking the stream, you have two options: move it or go around it. Bullies are like larger rocks. Thus, you must either move the rock or go around it.

3. Deal with bullies directly.

Confront bullies head-on—that is, move the rock. Avoiding confrontation leads to resentment. Resentment then sours relationships. If you don't confront bullies, the ministry will slow down, perhaps even come to an abrupt halt. In time, others in the congregation will get tired of the church bully, but it usually falls to the pastor to "do something about it."

As a solo pastor, you'll either have short-term pain and long-term gain or short-term gain and long-term pain. If you confront a bully, it'll be painful, but you'll get it out of the way, and in the long term the church will be better off. If you put off confronting a bully, you'll have gain in the short term, but pain will continue in the long term. In most situations it's better to confront sooner rather than later. Being betrayed, badgered, or belittled brings enormous pain—don't allow it to continue. Church bullies are able to sniff out weakness and fear of confrontation in others. When they detect such vulnerabilities, they are empowered to exert their own controlling behavior even more. Be courageous. Step up and confront the bully. Look at the courage of Joshua (Josh. 1:6–7, 9, 18) and the confidence of Peter and John (Acts 4:13). They served in different times, but the same Lord desires courage and confidence in his pastors today. Like someone once said, "If you have to eat some frogs, eat the big ones first." Confront the big bullies first and the smaller ones will hop away.

4. Attack problems, not people.

Work to separate the bully as a person from the issues. This may not be possible, as bullies merge so closely with some issues that they can't be separated. However, do your best to love the person while addressing the problem. One way to do this is to maintain respect for the bully as a person. Even if they use cutting words and are boisterous and mean-spirited, relate to them with standard courtesy. Resist mirroring their attitude or reactions. Be "shrewd as serpents and innocent as doves" (Matt. 10:16).

Hold them accountable by asking direct questions. For example, "How was this decision made?" "Who specifically are the other people who are concerned?" "Can you respond to the rumor that you've been spreading lies?" Then wait and let them

> *Confronting church bullies is not for the faint of heart, and it can be taxing mentally, relationally, and even physically on church leaders. Healthy churches and healthy church leaders, though, are not controlled by bullies, and whatever the price it's always worth the cost to break free.*
>
> —*Jonathan Davis*

respond. If this occurs in a board or business meeting, perhaps others will also raise questions. However, if no one speaks up but you, that's okay. It may take several confrontations before others gain the courage to say much. By all means, don't try to humiliate the bully. If they try to humiliate you, let the others see what the bully is really like, but respond only with kindness. Point out that your concern is for the church and Christ's honor rather than your own reputation.

5. If you can't confront a bully head-on, go around them.

One wise pastor suggests, "If you can't remove them, box them in." By this he means to take away their power. He relates how he asked the chairperson of his trustees to discuss a proposal with the entire committee. Later on, the pastor discovered that the chairperson had exerted control by not even presenting the proposal to the trustee committee. Rather than confront the chairperson directly at the following trustee meeting, which took place a month later, the pastor showed up unannounced. Walking around the table where the trustees sat, he greeted each one and handed each a copy of his proposal. Before he left, he told the entire group he needed them to review his proposal and give him an answer the following day. This action put the chairperson in a box where he had to review the proposal, since all the board members knew about the pastor's request. By doing this, the pastor went around the rock and sent a message that he was not going to allow the chairperson to exert control as a bully.

6. Realize that you'll make some major mistakes.

Sometimes you'll be misunderstood, say things that aren't appropriate, or generally screw up. Some mistakes can be overcome just by uttering the words "I'm sorry. I made a mistake. Can you forgive me?" These words are some of the most powerful you can ever say. Admitting the mistake and asking for forgiveness won't solve the problem. You'll need to rebuild trust and take care of the issue. Personal critique and attack normally push us into a mode of protectionism. As a pastor, you must look for the truth in the critique, embrace it, and move forward.

7. If a bully threatens to resign, accept their resignation.

Church bullies often threaten to resign as another means of control. They likely have used such a threat in the past, but prior pastors were too scared to call their bluff. If this happens, call their bluff! Immediately accept their resignation. Say something like "I'm sorry to hear this, but I respect your desire and accept your resignation. I'll let the board know today." Your response will shock the bully, as no one before was strong enough to deal with their threats. Occasionally, the bully will call the following day (or maybe right away) and try to take back their resignation. Don't allow them to do it. Hold your ground. Refuse to reconsider. They resigned. That's it. This may result in their leaving the church, and if they are part of a larger family group, you may see numerous people leave with them. Standing up to a bully is always risky, but even if they leave, it's worth the risk.

8. Control your mood from person to person and meeting to meeting.

This is easier said than done, of course. But after speaking with a bully, remember that the next person you encounter won't have knowledge of that experience. If you allow your emotions—anger, resentment, hurt—to carry over to the next person or meeting, it may damage relationships unnecessarily. The next meeting may be positive. Don't sabotage it with your bad feelings. When you feel rage or disgust, you may become focused and move rapidly in making decisions. This may work for you, but it also contains a danger in that rash and harsh comments may be spoken and unwise decisions made.

9. *Discover and speak the truth.*
Make it your goal to acquire the truth about any comments or assertions. Constantly ask people for the facts, not just rumor or opinion. Make finding and speaking truth a part of the church culture. When criticism is dispensed, be ready to push it back upstream to the source, and then deal with it directly and expeditiously. Do not fall into the trap of thinking, *If I do this one thing, the criticism will stop.* What you do will soon become an expectation, and the bully will find something else to be unhappy about. Bullies are only temporarily satisfied. Some may go underground for a brief time, but they'll be back with other attempts to exert their control.

Paul encourages all believers to speak "the truth in love" and, "laying aside falsehood, speak truth each one of you" (Eph. 4:15, 25). "A big transition that I have made," wrote an experienced solo pastor, "is to reframe my view of those who are bullies. I'm trying to take firm steps to keep a safe emotional distance between me and them, and yet to remain relationally connected, honest, candid, and loving with them. I'm trying to see their behavior as not directed at me as much as communicating their own desires, frustrations, and, more importantly, emotional underdevelopment. This helps me to speak truth without antagonism or defensiveness and helps me to care better for them."

10. *Realize that as a solo pastor, you may create your own conflict.*

This happens when you think you have to solve problems and fix situations at the church. Before trying to fix people or the church, consider it your job to know the people. Do not base actions and decisions on unexpressed or unexplored expectations founded on unexamined assumptions. Find out as much as possible about a bully's background. Were they hurt by a previous pastor? Was their family of origin difficult? Hurting people tend to hurt people, so try to discover the pain in the bully's life that causes them to hurt others.

11. Do not share information just because someone wants it.
You can divert questions without being rude. Your goal when dealing with gossips and tattletales is to respond amiably while revealing nothing of importance. If they ask what you're doing, say something like "Oh, just another boring project." If they keep pressing for more information, reply, "It's really not very interesting." Keep giving general answers until they stop asking. If people ask for information about other people, the best response is to be clueless. "I really have no idea" and "I don't know anything about that" are good answers.

12. Criticize others privately and praise them publicly.
This is a well-known approach but one that is easily forgotten. In an emotional moment it's easy to criticize, but if this is done in public, the effects are detrimental. Praise out loud; criticize quietly.

Don't make any ultimatums in public. If you find the need to make demands, do so individually or in a small group setting. If you need to ask a bully to step down from a position in the church, it's best to do so through your board or with one or two board members. You want the bully to know that you've taught your board how to handle bullies biblically. However, sometimes you must act alone. One pastor led a church to unprecedented growth over a ten-year period. During those years, one bully constantly criticized every decision, program, or action the pastor took to lead the church in a new direction. One Sunday following the worship service, the bully approached the pastor as he stepped down from the platform to the main floor. Again, he launched into a diatribe of criticism regarding the new style of worship, the pastor's attire, and the sermon. The pastor listened quietly, but when the bully was finished, the pastor said, "Let's sit down in the front pew for a moment." After sitting, the pastor continued, "You don't like our church, do you?" to which the bully replied, "No! I don't." With love and courage, the pastor replied, "Well, I don't like you being here either. So, let's pray, and then you can leave the church and not come back." Immediately, the pastor bowed his head and prayed a short prayer, asking the Lord to help the bully find a new church where he'd be happier. After saying amen, the pastor stood up, shook hands with the bully, and walked away, leaving him standing alone. The exchange took place quietly, with no one else aware of what had happened. The bully left the church, and the atmosphere has been much healthier ever since.

SOLO PASTORS LEAD churches that quite often include a significant number of people who are related to one another. When a church has 15 percent or more people from the same family, it can be quite difficult to lead. If the percentage of people related to one another is above 15 percent, more than likely a few of the family members wield major influence and power. Members of the family may deny they have any control, and in truth they may not see it. Or they may camouflage their control in spiritual language. You will see their control when most of the teams, committees, or leadership roles include one or more of the influential family members.

Do not assume that personal relationships within the church are what they seem. Members of the controlling family are more important than the pastor or other outsiders, even if the family knows some of its members are bullies. A dysfunctional family undermines the solo pastor every time, and they usually make the pastor the scapegoat. Issues in a dysfunctional family system found in solo-pastor churches should be dealt with biblically and substantively at the board level, at the constituency level, and both personally and professionally. It may take an outsider, perhaps a denominational leader or independent consultant, to bring about lasting change.

THREE QUESTIONS

1. Have you ever been the target of a bully or observed one in action? If so, share what you've seen.
2. Which of the bullying tactics mentioned in this chapter have you experienced or observed in a church?
3. What are the best ways to deal with bullies that you've seen or heard about?

TWO IDEAS

1. Do some study on how to check bullies, and then train your board and other church leaders so they are prepared to deal with such people if and when they become vocal.
2. Ask other pastors to share stories of how they dealt with bullies in their churches. Start making a list of ways to check them in your own church.

PART 3

The Solo Pastor Takes Charge

SEVEN

Communicate Well

A crisis creates a leaky bucket of communications. The tap needs to be fully opened.

—Bob Wriedt

I really appreciate our times together," Bill commented. "Your perspective has helped me gain a better understanding of my church."

"That's good to hear," Jim acknowledged. "What shall we talk about today?"

"I'm not sure what you'd call it. So, let me explain it this way," Bill continued. "I was disappointed in the attendance at a recent event our church scheduled. I advertised the event in our church program for a month and announced it from the pulpit every Sunday. However, attendance was very low. Afterward, I asked a few people why they didn't come and was told they didn't hear about it. Others said they heard about it too late to get it on their schedules."

"Okay, tell me more about this," Jim inquired.

"I talked it over with some board members. Some think people are just making up excuses for a lack of commitment, but a few others think there may be some truth in what they're saying—that is, they didn't hear about it. Our church is relatively small, and I think anyone can keep up with our church schedule if they even halfway try."

"You said the event was announced from the pulpit and in the church program, right?"

"Yes, that's right."

"Did you communicate the event in any other ways?"

"Well, no. I guess we didn't. I just assumed everyone would get the message."

"Let's think this through a bit," Jim suggested as he started drawing on a napkin. He sketched a church and next to it the caricature of a person. "Let's brainstorm a moment together. What ways can or does your church communicate to people?"

"I already mentioned announcements and the church program," Bill noted. "But we also have a Facebook page, and we can send texts to those we have phone numbers for."

Jim dutifully jotted the words *announcements*, *program*, *Facebook*, and *text* under his picture of a church. Then he drew a line toward the person he'd drawn. "Any other ways you can think of mentioning?" he asked.

"Oh, we also put up posters advertising the event, one near the restrooms as I recall."

"Those are all good," Jim began, "but it's really not enough."

"Not enough?" Bill looked puzzled. "Jim, my church is not that large. I communicated the event three ways, and come to think of it, it should also have been passed around via the church's grapevine, so that makes four different ways it was communicated."

"I know that sounds like enough," Jim agreed. "But it's really not. I recently read that the average person in the United States receives up to ten thousand messages per day. But here's the crazy news. Of those messages, only about 100, or fewer than 1 percent, are remembered.[1] So even if you delivered, say, twelve hundred messages during your four weeks of announcements, only about twelve of them—1 percent—were effectively received and remembered."

"Communicating well really is complex, isn't it?" Bill stated as he thoughtfully processed the conversation.

COMMUNICATING IS A RESPONSE to the human need to know. Preaching from the pulpit on Sundays is just the beginning of the solo pastor's need to communicate well. Every word uttered by the solo pastor has meaning to those in the congregation, even words spoken privately. At first glance, it appears that communication in a solo-pastor church is fairly easy. Such churches are usually small, so the lines of communication should be clear. An in-depth look at communication, however, reveals that even in solo-pastor churches, communication is complex. Consider the following insights.

1. Solo-pastor churches have multiple communication channels.
Some people receive information via the proverbial grapevine. Others are outside the grapevine loop and never get the information as it's passed from person to person. They get their information from looking at posted announcements on the church's website. If the website is not updated on a regular basis—say, weekly—they do not receive the messages in a timely manner. Some listen for announcements during the church's worship service. Others gain information through communication channels such as Twitter, Facebook, Instagram, email, texts, newsletters, pastoral visits, lay visits, phone calls, special mailings, and so on. At minimum, every church has thirty or more channels through which it communicates with the congregation.

2. The grapevine is fast but not always accurate.
Someone hears something, then passes it along to another person, who in turn passes it along to still another person until numerous people have heard. This is the one type of communication that

is found in every church, regardless of size. In general, the larger the congregation and the more geographically scattered people are, the less accurate the communication that travels through the grapevine.

3. Some people will not get the message.

Even with so many communication channels available, it's best to assume that some people in the church will not receive messages. One-way communication that doesn't include the possibility of feedback is likely to be overlooked. An announcement is sent out, but there is no way to know how many people receive the message.

4. Some people will receive the message but not understand it.

Some messages get garbled in transmission, while others are not as clear as the originator intended them to be. This is especially the case when communication is delivered by social media. Messages sent electronically are prone to misinterpretation and misunderstanding due to the lack of being able to see body language or hear inflections in the tone of voice. It's easy to miss the intended emotion and attitude of the sender.

5. Some people will receive the message, understand it, but not remember it.

Even with the best communication, people forget. Received communication is laid aside, misplaced, or forgotten in today's

> *A reasonably safe rule is that in most congregations every important message from the church to the people should be sent on five different channels.*
>
> *—Lyle E. Schaller*

busy world. Each person is bombarded with thousands of messages every day. This is overwhelming for most people.

6. *Some people receive a message that was never sent.*

People tend to hear what they want to hear. Thus, even the clearest words are often misinterpreted by listeners. For example, a pastor may think they're approaching a topic in love, but people hear law instead.

7. *Silence does not mean acceptance.*

Even though members of the congregation may hear and understand a message correctly, this doesn't mean they agree with it. Too often, a lack of disagreement is taken to mean that people agree, which isn't true. Don't assume silence is agreement.

8. *Two-way communication is better than one-way.*

A person-to-person phone call is better communication than a one-way text, for example. Any communication that allows for immediate feedback is best. Thus, person-to-person communication (a luncheon meeting, for example) is better than object-to-person communication (an email, for example).

9. *The importance of a message is determined by the recipient.*

Communication that begins with the recipient's interests, concerns, or problems in mind is more likely to be read, understood, and remembered than communication that begins with the sender's interests, concerns, or problems.

10. *Messages communicated multiple times and in multiple ways are more likely to be effective.*

The law of repetition says, "Communicating a message multiple times in multiple ways increases the probability that it will be received with a minimal degree of distortion." The law of redundancy says, "Communicating a message in the same way over and over again increases the probability that the message will be learned." Both repetition and redundancy are necessary for effective communication. Redundancy is in view when a congregation repeats its purpose statement every Sunday morning. In time, every person will remember the church's purpose statement in its exact wording. Repetition is in view when an event is announced multiple times using different words and in different ways. A good rule is to communicate important messages five ways. This doesn't mean sending a message five times by email, for example, but rather sending it through five different channels of communication. Communicate every important message with both redundancy and repetition.

11. Different people require different channels of communication.
Channels that reach people in your congregation don't normally work to reach people outside your church (churched versus unchurched). Those that reach active members don't always reach inactive ones (churched versus dropouts). Some communication channels are appropriate for some messages but not for others (members versus nonmembers). The best way to determine which communication channels work best is to ask recipients how they heard about a church event. By questioning twenty-five people in a given category—for example, seniors, college students, or newcomers— you'll discover the right channels to use for different people.

"LET'S PROBE THE COMMUNICATION problem a bit deeper," Jim advised. "You should also be aware of the hidden message syndrome."

"I've never heard of that," replied Bill. "What do you mean?"

"Let me give you an illustration," Jim suggested. "A few years back a couple approached me in the parking lot as I walked to my car after the Sunday morning service. They shared some concerns about the children's program with me. I didn't say much, just smiled and nodded my head to indicate I heard them. Unfortunately, they heard a message I never sent. They understood my smile and nodding to mean I agreed with them and would do something about their concerns. Since I didn't do anything about them, they thought I had lied to them and they eventually left the church."

"That doesn't seem fair," Bill commented.

"I know," Jim agreed, "but it points out the fact that the church is filled with nonverbal messages. Here's another example from a time our church went through a financial downturn. We weren't able to give our staff much of a raise for the new budget year. I explained the situation to my secretary, and I thought everything was okay. However, two weeks later she resigned. Later I heard that she had interpreted the lack of a raise to mean she wasn't appreciated. Of course, I never meant to indicate she wasn't appreciated, but that was the message she heard.

"Let me give you one more example. In my first church I encountered a situation where an older lady was directing the children's program. I found out she'd been leading the program for eleven years. In conversations with her, she indicated she was tired and wanted some younger women to take over. I worked diligently to find her some help, and I found two younger women who joined her. Over the next year, the younger women helped the children's program triple in size. During that time the older lady dropped out of the program, and she later left the church. She never said anything, but I heard that the reason she left the church was that she felt she wasn't needed any longer. It was a nonverbal message that no one intended to send."

"I understand what you're describing," Bill noted. "What can I do about it?"

THE STORIES TOLD ABOVE are commonplace in solo-pastor churches. Nonverbal messages are sent and received regularly, for the most part unnoticed. The phenomenon is complicated in that messages are received that were never sent (Pastor Jim's secretary, for example), and other messages are sent but are not received (Pastor Jim's encounter in the parking lot, for example). Here are some constructive ways to respond to the hidden message syndrome.

1. *Recognize the tendency of people to hear messages that are not sent.*

The hidden message syndrome is a reality of life. It occurs in all forms of communication, whether in church, home, school, business, or politics. We can all recall instances when messages were received that we didn't intentionally send. Recognizing this tendency is a good start to better communication. Increase your own sensitivity to the existence of hidden messages.

2. *Explain the messages that are not being sent.*

Instead of simply smiling and nodding his head, Pastor Jim could have explained, "I appreciate your concern, but you need to speak to the children's program director." By speaking directly, he would have removed the tendency for the couple to hear an unintended hidden message behind his smile. Or, when speaking to his secretary, he could have added, "I know it's a disappointment not to receive a better raise, but I want you to know I really appreciate you and your work."

3. *Ask how people are feeling or what they are thinking.*

Two-way communication is crucial to eliminate hidden messages. Jim could have spoken with the older children's program director to see how she felt about the growth of the program under the younger women's direction. He simply could have asked, "I've noticed the children's program has grown. How do you feel about it?"

4. *Probe for second thoughts later on.*

It's odd, but most people don't respond with their true feelings or thoughts in the first moments of hearing a message. People need time to think and process their feelings. It's wise, then, to provide an opportunity for people to share their second thoughts. For example, after telling his secretary about the lower raise, Jim

> *At the core of effective leadership is the ability to communicate. All forms of communication must be mastered by the effective leader: Written and oral, electronic and digital, communication by graphics and behavior, by art and music, by expressed emotion and more.*
>
> —*Warren Wilhelm*

could have waited a week and then asked again how she was feeling. This would have given her time to process her thoughts and feelings and articulate them well.

5. Watch for changes in people's behavior.

Hidden messages—good and bad—are accompanied by changes in behavior. A family that was regular in worship attendance but now comes rarely is sending a hidden message. A person who has decreased their financial support is sending a hidden message. An individual who served faithfully but no longer serves is sending a hidden message. Hidden messages can also be positive. A person who suddenly starts attending services more frequently is sending a hidden message. A person who expresses a desire to serve is sending a hidden message. A family that increases their level of financial support is sending a hidden message. The question is, how will a solo pastor respond to these messages?

6. Don't confuse understanding and agreement.

Decide what you want before you try to communicate: understanding or agreement? The greater the understanding, the more chance there is of disagreement, but the greatest harm comes from disagreement without understanding. Great understanding with disagreement is not harmful. It's best to strive for understanding.

7. Realize that communication is the responsibility of leadership. Communication that creates understanding is a leadership concern. Failure to communicate well is indeed a failure of leadership. Thus, the responsibility to create understanding rests solely with the leader who communicates.

COMMUNICATION IS A VITAL concern for solo pastors. With so much advertising noise (ten thousand messages a day!) bombarding people, it's easy for church communication to be overlooked or forgotten. It's best to assume that people will not receive church messages without intentional effort by leaders to communicate multiple times, in multiple ways, on multiple channels.

THREE QUESTIONS

1. Is communication a problem in your church? If so, share some examples of how communication has gone awry.
2. How many channels of communication can you identify in your church? How many do you use intentionally?
3. Which of the ideas mentioned in this chapter will you try to use in the next few months?

TWO IDEAS

1. Conduct an informal survey among various groups in your church to determine which communication channels they listen to. Consider interviewing people who are newcomers, older saints, teenagers, college students, young singles, young marrieds, and so forth. Maintain a list of which communication channels work best for

each group, and begin to use those channels for better communication.

2. Analyze your last major church event. How many different communication channels were used? How much repetition was employed? How can you do a better job of communicating next time?

EIGHT

Establish Direction

Leaders have their head in the clouds and their feet on the ground.
—James M. Kouzes and Barry Z. Posner

Jim, I've benefited a great deal from our conversations over the last few months. Your insights on relationships, difficult people, and communicating are helpful. Which brings me to another question."

"I appreciate your kind words," Jim affirmed. "So, what's on your mind?"

"I've been putting into practice some of your suggestions from our previous conversations, yet it feels like my church is going nowhere. Everyone seems happy with the church just as it is."

"They're pretty comfortable?"

"Yes, comfortable is one word for it, but I think there's an overall lack of direction. There's another church in a nearby community that has the same theology as mine, is located in a similar neighborhood, and offers the same basic programs." Bill paused.

"But?"

"But it's growing and mine isn't."

"Why do you think that is?" Jim questioned.

"The only thing I can think of is it has a vision and my church doesn't. Last year I attended a seminar on 'Leading a Missional Church.' The speaker stressed the importance of having a vision for the future. After returning, I put together a retreat with my board to develop our vision. One of the board members suggested we adapt a vision statement he'd seen online from a successful church, and we soon came up with a nice statement. Since then, I've preached on our vision, we hung a banner in our worship center with our statement on it, and we placed the statement prominently on the first page of our website. But not much has happened. No one mentions our vision statement any longer. Even my board members don't reference it when making decisions. Looking back, it seems like our retreat was a waste of time. It's a good statement, it really is, but my church still lacks direction."

"What else have you tried in order to set direction for the church?"

"When I first started," Bill continued, "I talked a lot about becoming a missional church. I really believe we should *be* the church rather than just *do* church. The board especially liked what I had to say, and I initially thought it would be easy to set a new direction. My hopes didn't pan out. To *be* the church, I suggested we begin to serve the people in our neighborhood through acts of service. The first time we scheduled something for the neighbors, a few people from the church helped me, but each succeeding time we did some form of service, fewer and fewer people came out to help. I've been trying to build friendships with some neighbors, but the board doesn't help. The last time I talked to the board about this, they indicated they supported my efforts, but no one ever helps out. It's like the members say, 'Sure, pastor. Whatever you want to do is fine. We'll support you from as far away as possible.' They never say I can't do something, but neither do they help. So, where do I go from here? How do I bring my church and ministry into clearer focus and vitality?"

"Sounds like you're still a bit confused."

"You could say that. Even with all the good insights you've given me, I still wonder which way I should go. For instance, there are so many different approaches to ministry—missional church, church growth, church renewal, center church, and others—you name it. There are so many options I don't know which way to turn. How do I decide?"

BILL'S FRUSTRATION POINTS to a number of challenges facing solo pastors as they seek to establish direction for a local church. Following are seven observations and seven suggestions for setting direction in a solo-pastor church.

Seven Observations

1. *Establishing direction for a church is more complex than simply writing a vision statement.*

Recent publications have emphasized the importance of developing a vision statement for a church, and rightly so. However, a vision statement is only part of a larger concept. Much more than a vision is needed to set direction for a church. It also takes patience, tenacity, gentle persuasion, good communication, and, most of all, time to see a new direction established.

2. *You can't rent a vision.*

Borrowing a vision statement from a successful church may seem like a good idea at first. However, it's akin to renting a car. While the car is nice, it's not yours. You don't own it! Effective vision statements are owned by the congregation, not just rented. One church's heartbeat is never the heartbeat of another church.

3. *The concept of vision lacks clarity.*

Even when vision is treated as significant, it assumes an undefined content, left to be filled in by the audience. Expressed

> *The pastor, as a visionary, is like an architect who intimately knows each room in the building he or she is designing long before it's actually constructed.*
>
> —*Leith Anderson*

differently, an illusion of communication is present in the word *vision.* When a person hears that word, they think they know what it means but rarely do. More problematic, each hearer fills in the content differently, according to their own perceptions, assumptions, and biases. However, to some the mere word *vision* is problematic, and they are reluctant to embrace the concept, feeling it is too closely associated with some form of mysticism, like dreams or trances. Some aspects of this type of vision occurred in the Bible, of course. One only has to think about Moses's encounter at the burning bush (Exod. 3), Peter when he saw the sheet lowered from heaven (Acts 10), or Paul's story of being caught up into heaven (2 Cor. 12). Others see the concept of vision as consistent with God's way of revealing himself to chosen leaders. They expect that God entrusts to church leaders what he desires. To many people, the concept of vision is not something they think about. Left undefined, it is too general a term to be understood.

4. *A solo pastor must take responsibility for developing a church's vision.*

In part, this means creating an island of clarity in a sea of confusion. It's best to assume that formal and informal leaders in the church don't know how to set direction. It's extremely rare for a board or committee to determine a church's vision. Thus, it falls to the solo pastor to nudge them along toward the future. In reality, 85 percent of a solo pastor's leadership involves the ability to (1) set direction (what to do next), (2) organize people (get the right people in the right place), and (3) align resources (bring appropriate resources to bear on the plan). Another way to say this is that a solo pastor must know what God wants done next (direction), whom God wants to do it (organization), and how to use God's resources (application). While occasionally God gives direction to a group of people, in most occurrences throughout the Bible he gives direction to a single person, who then is given the responsibility to communicate it to the rest of the people. In solo-pastor churches, this usually means the pastor (although it sometimes is a gifted layperson).

5. Setting direction is a process, not an event.

The congregation may not articulate this, but they sense a need for a vision and a plan for the future. It takes more than a weekend retreat, however, to establish a new direction for a local church. A planning retreat can be helpful, but it's only part of the process, not its entirety. Setting direction takes an ongoing commitment to hard work as well as regular communication, evaluation, and retooling, to name a few things not often talked about. No one should attempt to set a new direction for a church unless they're willing to commit to a minimum of three years of hard work, sometimes longer.

6. When you provide a clear TRACK combined with ACTION, you get TRACTION.

Many solo-pastor churches have lost all sense of direction, particularly if they have been through a crisis. During a crisis, church leaders tend to turn inward, focusing solely on survival rather than expansion. They become directionless. What solo-pastor churches then do is solve problems rather than plan for the future. A better way to look at problems is to see them as opportunities to readjust the church's direction.

Plans are like a railroad track on which a train runs. Without the track, the train would go nowhere. Then, too, if the track is in place but the engine doesn't take action, the train just sits there. Having a track without action or action without a track leads to distraction (spinning of wheels). That's a picture of some churches. Either they have no plan (track) or they have a plan but can't get moving to fulfill it (no action). Both lead to the church being distracted from its main mission of reaching the lost for Christ. But with a track and action, the church can gain traction and move forward.

7. You can't plan forever.

An old proverb says, "He who deliberates fully before taking a step will spend his entire life on one leg." Church leaders taking too long to establish new direction happens so frequently that this is almost a proverb: "Church leaders who deliberate fully before taking action will spend their entire life in committee." An average plan put into action is better than an excellent plan left undone. The point is to get moving and let God direct your steps along the way (see Prov. 16:9).

Seven Suggestions

1. Form a team to develop a master plan.

A board or committee seldom thinks about establishing a master plan on its own. In solo-pastor churches, though, involving the key leaders on a planning team is needed to create ownership. This team is most often the board. You can also involve other people by invitation, and it's wise to include key influencers if you desire for the plan to gain traction. Godly character of the people on the team is foundational but not sufficient. Determine what type of experience is needed to accomplish the potential plan. If you hope to build a new facility, for instance, try to include someone on the team who has experience in that area. Members of your planning team will tend to project their own experiences onto the church. If they are struggling financially, for example, their situation may cloud their judgment regarding the church's ability to meet the financial obligations of the plan. If they don't have personal dreams and goals, they may have difficulty envisioning the plan and its completion.

2. Talk to God.

The idea of a master plan reveals two key concepts. One, it is a *master* plan—that is, a plan informed by what the Master, Jesus Christ, desires for his church. Two, it's a master *plan*—that is, the steps your church will follow for the next few years.

Keep in mind that Jesus said, "I will build My church" (Matt. 16:18). This means he has a plan for every local church. Since he is "head over all things to the church" (Eph. 1:22), it's reasonable to ask him to reveal his plan for your local church. So begin the process of setting direction by asking in prayer for Jesus Christ to reveal his plan to you and the other leaders on your team. Vision begins with a holy discontent with the way things are or a holy passion for the way things ought to be. Of course, both can work simultaneously. Discovering the holy discontent or passion comes through being together, spending time in prayer, and answering to the best of your ability questions such as "What does God want for our church in the coming three years?" One way to answer this question is to make a list of the needs you observe in the ministry area around your church. For example, you might note that families are searching for reliable childcare or seeking tutors for their children, or that couples are struggling with finances. List as many needs as you can observe. Then compare the list to the people in your church. Do you have people with expertise in any of the areas of need? If you do, perhaps this is the direction God wants your church to head. If you see needs but have no one with the skills to address them, it's likely that God is not guiding you in that direction. Write down what you believe God is saying, even if you don't have a clear answer. Just get your ideas down on paper, as sometimes the process of writing helps bring clarity of direction.

3. Study the church's history.

Churches have personality, and, as with individuals, the past impacts their present and future. Work with the members of your team to complete a study of your church in four phases. Phase 1: Look at the church's history. Go all the way back to the founding of the church. What were the major events, turning points, and decisions that still affect the church? This reveals the DNA or core values that have impacted the church throughout the years. Phase 2: Chart the last ten years of worship attendance. If it's helpful, you can also chart the last decade of one or two other aspects of the church, such as small group involvement, membership, number of baptisms, and so on. Chart no more than two or three, as that is all you need to understand the trend of your church's health. Phase 3: Take a keen look at the charts. What trends do you see? What questions arise? Phase 4: Analyze the church's direction. If things remain the same, what direction do the trends point to for your church? Trends tend to continue unless intentional effort is made to change them. Consider the impact of either stopping what's not working or at least redirecting resources to what's working.

4. Investigate the needs of the church and community.

At this point, divide your master planning team into two groups: a P team and an F team. P stands for present and F stands for future. Assign the P team to study the present church. What is working well? What is not working well? What needs to be accomplished in the coming three years to improve the present church ministries? In short, this team completes an audit of the present church and makes recommendations for improvement. Then assign the F team to study the future of the church. How is the community around the church changing? What will be the future needs of the unchurched in your community? What does the church need to change to be fruitful in the next three years? In short, this team looks at the future and makes recommendations on what the church must do to be relevant in the next three years.

5. *Complete a KWIKN (pronounced "quicken") analysis.*

Gather the entire planning team together and ask the P team and the F team to make presentations to the entire team. Following both presentations, do the KWIKN (Knowing What I Know Now) analysis: Knowing what we know now, what do we want to do in the coming three years? This one major question can be enlarged by asking, "What do we want to start doing? What should we stop doing? What changes must we make to be fruitful in the next three years?" Don't share your own conclusions with the teams. Allow them to go through the process themselves.

6. *Write a master plan.*

Once you've done the praying, the studying, and the analyzing, you can begin to write a master plan. It should include a statement of purpose (What is the biblical reason our church exists?); a statement of vision (What do we hope to accomplish?); and a statement of goals (What are we specifically going to do?). A pivotal statement at this point in the process is "Assuming the blessing of God on our church, in three years we hope to see X, Y, and Z." These become your goals. Lastly, and this is crucial, develop a plan that nonbusiness people can work with and understand. The average person in your church should be able to say, "This makes sense." Solo-pastor churches do not function well with a complex plan, no matter how good it may appear on paper. The old adage "Keep it simple" is applicable.

As leaders we recognize that we are all prisoners of our hope. Our hope sustains us. Our vision of what could be inspires us and those we lead.

—C. William Pollard

7. Align resources with the goals.

The major resources available to a church are prayer, people, and money. Once your team has written the basic master plan, add to each goal the name of the person who is going to pray for it to be accomplished, the person who is going to do it, and the amount of money from the budget they have to spend on it. If possible, always assign a person rather than a committee or group to be responsible to get the goal accomplished. Groups, like committees, are good at talking about things but not so good at getting things done.[1]

A Word about the Board

As Bill explained in the conversation at the beginning of this chapter, the board agreed to let him do whatever he wanted, but they didn't help out. This type of attitude can be understood from several different angles.

(1) In solo-pastor churches, the board is often tasked with controlling a pastor, not empowering them. When a church has suffered much hurt from previous pastors, it may place all decision-making authority within the board in an effort to protect the church from further trauma. By requiring the solo pastor to obtain permission before launching anything new, they hope to keep anything from taking place that will put the church in jeopardy.

(2) The nature of solo-pastor churches means the board is a decision-making board rather than an executive board. Decision-making boards meet regularly to complete the three Ds: discuss, determine, and decide all courses of action for the entire church. Even if they trust the solo pastor, they still expect to make all the decisions. In contrast, an executive board sets broad policies while allowing the pastor (and other staff if there are any) to make most of the day-to-day, week-to-week, month-to-month, and year-to-year decisions. However, an executive board is not often found in solo-pastor churches.

(3) Some churches view group decisions as a major aspect of their theology. They reason that since the Holy Spirit resides in all true believers, all believers must have a say in all decisions within the church. For some churches, this requires regular all-church business meetings, but for others, regular board meetings will suffice.

(4) Other churches see the board model as the only biblical one, citing most often Acts 6:1–7, where the disciples appear to act as the board of the church in Jerusalem. If this model was good enough for the church in Jerusalem, it must be good enough for us too. For churches in democratically led countries, the decision-making board fits the culture quite nicely. They reason that it provides representation while keeping the pastor from becoming a dictator.

The hope for establishing a new direction increases when the solo-pastor church acknowledges the central importance of the board. A wise pastor works with the board as much as godly possible. (Normally, one might say "humanly" possible, but the Holy Spirit is at work to empower the solo pastor beyond what is humanly possible.)

If you are a solo pastor, remember that the board members can be great companions in ministry. It's a mistake to view the board members as difficult people. Most are significant leaders in the church and have been given their position due to faithful service over numerous years. They are legitimate leaders of the church and likely have deep connections to those not on the board.

When you are establishing direction, therefore, connect the board to the process. Not only must their ideas, insights, and opinions be taken into consideration, but the reality is that they must support the new direction and help communicate it to those within the larger church body if it is to succeed. Ephesians 4:11–12 indicates that pastors are to equip the saints for the work of ministry. For the solo pastor, the key saints they need to equip for service are the board members. If you are a solo pastor, your role is to be the leader among leaders, or the initiating leader. In this role, you assist the board in discovering the church's purpose, determining its vision, setting its goals, deciding its actions, and encouraging the people in pursuit of the overall direction of the church. All of this takes place in the midst of growing relationships of trust and mutual service to one another. Together, as you share ministry leadership as a team, you'll find support, love, care, and mutual joy.

In the process of establishing direction along with the board, a solo pastor could be called pastor-leader, or player-coach, or catalyst-encourager. All of these possible titles stress collaboration and joint effort. Solo pastors must move away from thinking they have to make all the decisions and create a collective alliance with board members. Purposeful relationships truly signal leadership maturity in the solo pastor.

THREE QUESTIONS

1. Is there a master plan for your church in place? Why or why not? If so, how do people perceive its effectiveness? Its validity? Its usefulness?
2. What is the board's understanding of its role in establishing direction? How does it fit with your understanding? What training or encouragement do board members need?
3. What barriers will you need to overcome to set a fresh direction for your church?

TWO IDEAS

1. As you meet with people, ask them to share their hopes and dreams for the church. Listen carefully, writing down ideas as they are shared. Take special notes on where, how, and among whom the Holy Spirit is working. Even in the

most difficult situations, God tends to be speaking to or stirring up to good works about 10 percent of the congregation. Who are the 10 percent? Identify them. Pray with them for the future spiritual and numerical growth of your church. Share ideas together.

2. Ask many questions of your leaders that naturally point them toward the future. Here are a few good questions:

- If our church could be all that God wants it to be, what would it look like?
- How is God already working in our community, and how can we join him?
- Where and when has God blessed our church in the past, and how can we reconnect with his blessing?
- What is our church's heartbeat?

NINE

Manage Resources

Faith doesn't send us charging into every possible ministry, reck-lessly squandering financial and human resources.

—David and Becky Waugh

There's one other item I'd like to discuss today," Bill com-mented as the previous discussion wound down. "It seems strange, but my church already has a vision statement—actually quite a big vision for the future. In my mind it's too big of a vision, but I hesitate to say that to my leaders."

"How so?" Jim inquired.

"The church's current vision statement says, 'Faith Church ex-ists to redeem all people, restoring them through gospel-centered preaching, baptizing them in the name of the Father, Son, and Holy Spirit, and teaching them to obey everything that Jesus taught in the Bible.'"

"That is pretty comprehensive," Jim admitted.

"I realize that having a vision is essential, but this is way more than my church can accomplish. On top of that, trying to fulfill it is burning my people out. This last year we held a two-week Vacation Bible School, hosted two youth teams from our denomination during the summer, and ran a full schedule of children's and youth events all year, including a snow retreat, ski week, summer camp, and fall festival. Along with all that, we had the normal adult programming, added a new worship service, and started a food ministry outreach to the low-income neighborhood near our church. It was so hectic that I'm sure people were avoiding me so they wouldn't get recruited for another project."

"I'll bet." Jim laughed. "I'd probably have avoided you too."

"It'd be funny if it wasn't so true," Bill concurred. "The people like the large vision, but, honestly, it's so broad that I think it's useless. If it was more specific, or maybe I should say focused, I think it'd be better all around. As it is, we tend to jump at any new idea for ministry that comes along because every new opportunity seems to fit our vision statement. We don't have a good way to prioritize what we're doing. Jim, there's a limit to what we can do. We just don't have enough people, energy, or money."

"I like what the paraphrase of Proverbs 24:3–4 says: 'Any enterprise is built by wise planning, becomes strong through common sense, and profits wonderfully by keeping abreast of the facts' [TLB]. Good stewardship of resources is akin to the two wings of an airplane—good planning is one wing and walking by faith is the other. Both wings are needed to get off the ground, fly, and return safely to the ground. God empowers us by faith, but he uses the resources he puts into our hands."

BILL AND JIM'S CONVERSATION reveals a common problem in solo-pastor churches and poses a deep question: How can a church balance faith and practice? Churches thrive on big vision (faith) but face the reality of limited resources (practice). Here are some insights and tips to consider.

1. Faith and practice are not enemies but partners in ministry. Vision and ministry fit together. A God-given vision requires a church to step forward in practical ways to connect with real people in ministry situations. Faith is needed to begin new ministries, but this implies strategic thought, not a blind leap. God's Word suggests that faith is best balanced with facts. Proverbs 18:13 is emphatic in this case: "He who gives an answer before he hears, it is folly and shame to him." A paraphrase is more explicit: "What a shame—yes, how stupid!—to decide before knowing the facts!" (TLB). When talking about discipleship, Jesus advised his followers to count the cost. "For which one of you, when he wants to build a tower, does not first sit down and calculate the cost to see if he has enough to complete it? . . . Or what king, when he sets out to meet another king in battle, will not first sit down and consider whether he is strong enough with ten thousand men to encounter the one coming against him with twenty thousand?" (Luke 14:28, 31). Solo pastors have an urge to lead a church beyond its capacity. As Christians, we must count the cost of discipleship, but the principle applies to ministry too—godly faith leads to strategically planned ministry.

2. Healthy churches are vision critical.
Proverbs 29:18 reminds leaders, "Where there is no vision, the people are unrestrained." This passage can be translated as the people "run wild" or "get out of hand." Unless the vision is defined so people can see not only where to go but also how to get there, they'll be running wild. A healthy church knows in which direction

> *We must have an understanding of what it's going to cost in money, facilities, and other types of energy, and we must have these resources available.*
>
> —*Edward R. Dayton*

it's heading. This requires that (1) people know, understand, and believe in the church's overall vision; (2) each person understands their place in fulfilling the vision; (3) people hear about the needs of the congregation and want to help; (4) victories and successes regarding the vision are shared with the congregation; (5) people hear about how the vision has changed lives; (6) communication channels are kept open and active; and (7) church leaders take responsibility to make certain the first six are done.

3. Solo-pastor churches have high hopes but few resources.

"Big vision, modest means" is a silent reality churches find difficult to manage. While a church doesn't wish to lower its dreams, it must strategically use the resources God has provided. This means sharpening the focus of the church on its primary resources: spiritual, people, facility, and money. Each of these resources overlaps the others, strengthening or weakening each one.

4. A solo-pastor church can start one major ministry a year.

A solo-pastor church can adequately add only one new ministry a year, and perhaps retool two other ministries. Hence, it's wise to consider if there are enough resources to complete any plan.

Ministry in a solo-pastor church requires that this question be asked and answered honestly: How far will our resources stretch? As with building a building or fighting a war, beginning a new ministry and then running short on resources will lead to failure. Too many failures in a solo-pastor church create a fear of taking future steps of faith. A shortage of resources doesn't close the door on new ministry, but it does mean serious effort must be given to weighing the resource demands and costs.

5. Recognize the church's limits and narrow your goals.

Leaping from the ground to a rooftop several stories high sounds exciting, but it's possible only among fictional superheroes. In most cases, the best way to get on a rooftop is to use a ladder to climb up one rung at a time. Recognizing your limits and narrowing your focus help define priorities. By setting measurable goals, like rungs on a ladder, you can step progressively higher and higher until you accomplish your vision. If the vision is too broad, it'll be like placing multiple ladders against numerous buildings. Which one do you climb first? Which is the most important? Which deserves the investment of time, personnel, and energy? With too many ladders to climb, you'll end up frustrated, with a sense of failure. You could do many good things this year, but you are not likely to do them all. Do one thing—then another the following year.

6. *Think of ministry as a long-distance run rather than a sprint.* Sprinters go all out, exhausting themselves in a short race to win. Contrary to sprinters, long-distance runners pace themselves to finish a longer distance. Doing too much too fast in a solo-pastor church brings overextension, disillusionment, and collapse. Exhaustion will likely result in a ministry project with insufficient strength to survive. Pace the church's ministries so your people don't burn out.

7. *Knock on doors of opportunity; enter open ones.* Don't give up on the larger, comprehensive vision, but invest your energy in meeting needs that match your present resources. Wait patiently for other dreams to materialize as the resources to run and maintain them are brought forth. "We had a lot of schoolteachers in our church," remembers one solo pastor. "They were always pushing us to start a Christian elementary school. After giving it consideration, the elders determined the resources weren't there for a full-blown elementary school but that we could manage to begin a preschool. We walked through that open door, and five years later the preschool was so successful that we were able to start building an entire elementary school."

8. *Deciding not to invest resources is not saying no, just "not yet."* Use two criteria to determine when to say yes and when to say no to new opportunities. (1) Do your people "own" the vision? If

it originated with one or a few, do others see it as a priority? It's best to delay starting a new ministry unless you have a minimum of five people committed to getting it started and keeping it running. (2) Do you have the emotional and spiritual resources, personnel, money, and facilities? If God gives the vision *and* the resources (or honest anticipation of resources), it's an automatic yes. If either one of these is missing, or if conditions are uncertain, it's a not yet.

9. Aim for the attainable.
There's a difference between possible and probable. It's always fun to think about the possibilities, but aiming for the probable is usually more helpful. Unrealistic expectations often set a congregation up for disappointment and frustration. If people have been misled before, or have experienced huge disappointments previously, they'll resist a new vision and taking hold of new opportunities.

10. Never be content with what you're doing.
A vision shouldn't allow you to be comfortable. A vision should recognize limitations but always stretch you to enlarge your boundaries. Holy discontent is living with a vision that you can't possibly attain—at least not yet!

11. Don't blow the bugle to gather your team too soon.
A military trumpet player signals the army to attack but also to retreat, to go to bed, and a number of other things. Paul observed, "If the bugle produces an indistinct sound, who will prepare himself for battle?" (1 Cor. 14:8). While Paul was talking about a different issue, blowing the bugle too soon occurs when (1) a good idea falls through; (2) too little communication has taken place; (3) ownership is not really there; (4) changing directions happens too soon and too fast; or (5) a vision is shared before defining and refining it.

12. If you don't measure it, it won't succeed.
Solo pastors tend not to like measuring aspects of ministry. This is unfortunate, because measuring resources is a must for fruitful ministry. It's easy to measure facilities, money, and personnel,

> *One major resource is the people who are going to do the work. Make a clear estimate of the hours that are going to be involved, and make certain, when you add up all of those hours, they do not exceed the number of hours available.*
>
> *—Ted W. Engstrom*

but you might be wondering, "How do you measure spiritual resources?" It's simple, actually: by looking at how many people are involved in prayer and engaged with God's Word (attending worship, involved in small group studies, reading the Bible, etc.). Are people concerned with the lost or only themselves? Is there a yearning for souls to be saved? How many nonchurched people are being prayed for this year? Assisting people to grow in spiritual maturity and measuring the extent of the growth lead to success.

13. Make spiritual resources God-centered and participant-focused.

The primary spiritual resources that all congregations have are God's Word, worship, and prayer. And in each of these areas, faith is empowered by centering on God and involving people. In part this means using a preaching style that is conversational—that is, talking to people rather than preaching at them. It also means giving worship back to the people by engaging them in singing rather than having them simply listen to the musicians on stage. Using new songs is nice, but the words, rhythms, and vocal range must fit the ability of the congregation. Renew the congregation's involvement with prayer. This may not take the form of the old traditional weeknight prayer meeting, but emphasize prayer in small groups, meetings, and anywhere you possibly can.

14. Recruit people to one major ministry a year.

Set a policy that people may serve in one major ministry role and one minor ministry role each year. You'll need to define which ministries are major and minor, but the main issue is time involvement. Average church attendees have less than three hours per week to volunteer. You must use their time wisely. Generally, any ministry that requires three hours of time involvement outside of Sunday worship is a major one.

15. Manage the money.

This topic is a big one, but try these ideas. (1) Guide the church to place reasonable controls on its finances. If the church doesn't have a budget, lead in creating one. (2) Divide up financial responsibilities between different family units. For example, those who count the money, deposit the money, and write checks should never be part of the same family unit. (3) Monitor cash flow weekly or monthly—that is, the fixed expenses, the income, and whether they balance. (4) Teach on the topic of stewardship at least once a year. People are hungry to know how to manage finances—their own and the church's. Don't shy away from preaching on appropriate passages about money found in the Bible.

AT THE TURN of the century in 1900, churches in the snowy north had long sheds. Each shed was closed in on the north, west, and east sides but open on the south. It was a place for church attendees to park their horses, buggies, and wagons while they attended church. With the advent of the automobile, by 1920 most of these sheds had been demolished to provide space for parking lots, though a few were left standing and converted into storage sheds. By the 1950s, the lots had been paved to provide a less messy walk for congregants from their cars into the church. Other changes have occurred over the last half century. For example, Sunday school has been replaced by small groups in a number of churches. More changes and adaptations are on the way. It's time to manage your church's resources in preparation for future demands, expectations, and opportunities.

THREE QUESTIONS

1. When a congregation is committed to too many foci, vision is diluted. What is the focus of your church's vision? Is it too broad or too narrow?
2. Our culture is becoming more visual-oriented than word-oriented. How do you visualize your vision to your congregation?
3. Stated in fewer than twenty-five words, where is your church headed in the next three years?

TWO IDEAS

1. Think about the resources available to your church: spiritual, people, money, facilities, and others. Which of them is a barrier to the future development of your church? Ask others in your church, and determine which is your weakest resource. Brainstorm ways to improve this resource, and take the first steps to enlarge it.
2. What are some new, major ministries your church could start if it had the resources to do so? Make a list of potential ministries that you've considered or that others have recommended. What open door is available to you now that might lead to being able to start one of those ministries later on? Rewrite your list of ministries in order of priority, and start looking for the resources you'll need to begin the first one.

PART 4

The Solo Pastor
Stays Healthy

TEN

Set Priorities

Parkinson's Law: Work expands to fill the time available for its completion.

—C. Northcote Parkinson

I need your help and input on how I can stay sane through this phase of my life and ministry."

"That sounds ominous, Bill. Anything particular going on I should know about?"

"Nothing ominous, Jim. Just me being frustrated, I guess. Like I said before, there are so many models or strategies or approaches to ministry being batted around these days that I'm totally confused about which direction to go or which model to use."

"I understand what you're saying. I've had some of the same frustrations the last few years. When I first started in ministry, the only model was that of a traditional shepherd who fed, protected, and cared for the sheep. In my first church, the people expected me to preach, care, and visit. That was about all they wanted. Now there are many more expectations placed on a pastor. I feel for you, and other pastors too."

"There are highly opinionated people in my church who really put the pressure on me to do ministry their way. Sometimes I agree with them, but other times what they want goes totally against what I believe my role is as a pastor. They're not bullies, like we talked about before, but just good people who are ambitious to give me direction. How do I set priorities in my life and ministry to help me in the coming years?"

IF A SOLO PASTOR doesn't know their own mind regarding the role of a pastor, the church members will give their views. Trying to go in several directions at once is never productive, and doing so will always be frustrating. The best way for a solo pastor to eliminate the frustrations of trying to meet others' expectations and to find a way forward is through setting priorities for their life and work. The following steps can help you establish boundaries and take some direct control.

1. Develop your LPOV (leadership point of view).

All pastors are visionaries to some extent. You wouldn't be in ministry without some form of vision—that is, a picture of what you'd like to see take place in the future. As you've moved forward in your life and ministry, you have followed a general pathway of where you think God wants you to go. That's your vision. As a companion to your journey, you've also developed a leadership point of view—that is, how you understand leadership and how it plays out in your ministry. What you likely haven't done is written it down.

A passage in Habakkuk 2 encourages the writing down of key concepts like vision and LPOV. The prophet was concerned about leaders oppressing the poor and questioned why God was not doing something about it. God told Habakkuk, "I am doing something in your days—You would not believe if you were told. For behold, I am raising up the Chaldeans" (1:5–6). Later, God told Habakkuk to "record the vision and inscribe it on tablets,

> *I want to be a warm and gentle pastor who comforts and the visionary pastor who challenges.*
>
> —*Jack Hayford*

that the one who reads it may run. For the vision is yet for the appointed time; it hastens toward the goal and it will not fail. Though it tarries, wait for it; for it will certainly come, it will not delay" (2:2–3). Note the importance of writing down the vision so that others can read it. There's something powerful about writing down your vision and your LPOV. As you refer to them on a regular basis, God will move you toward their fulfillment. Setting priorities begins with clarifying your identity. Where are you headed? What are your values? What is your viewpoint on how to lead?

When a solo pastor does not clarify their LPOV, they are left open to going in any direction and using any strategy to get there. As God told Habakkuk to do, a solo pastor must inscribe on paper, and on their heart and mind, their vision and LPOV. Here are some tips to help you determine your LPOV.

Know your strengths. Like everyone else, pastors have strengths and weaknesses. Spending inordinate amounts of time on things you do weakly, poorly, and inadequately creates an overall mess. The solo pastor is more effective when they work in areas that align with their strengths, but few solo pastors really know their strengths. To be a great solo pastor, you must learn to recognize your strengths and focus on them. On your computer or a pad of paper, note the areas or experiences in your life where you've sensed God's blessing. Where have you observed success or fruitfulness? Think back over your entire life, as strengths are often evident from a young age. Once you've narrowed down your areas of strength, try to focus your ministry to build on them.

Know your history. This means three things: you must know your personal history, know church history, and know your church's history.

Know your role. From your biblical study, what is your role as a pastor? The complexity of a solo pastor's job is compounded by the willingness of their church to let them do anything and everything. It's up to you to define your role and communicate it to the congregation.

Put your strengths, history, and role together to form your LPOV. Share it with others in your church so they come to understand your philosophy of ministry work.

2. Log your time.

At first thought, this may seem curious, but the more you're available to people, the less they will respect you. The reason? You won't be taking care of the crucial aspects of pastoring that need doing. One pastor reported a businessman commenting, "Why are you always here when I call? Don't you have more important things to do than hang around answering the phone?" Of all the resources available, time is the one that is not renewable. One can always find more money, property, and people, but once time is gone, it's gone—forever!

Fruitful solo pastors don't start with their tasks but with their time. They find out where their time is actually going, attempt to cut back the unproductive demands on their time, and group their discretionary time into blocks of activity. This takes a three-step process: recording time, identifying time-wasting activities, and consolidating time.

Record your actual time usage. The method you use to log your time is not important. Just do it for one week or one month (most pastors won't have the determination to log more than a week). Record every fifteen minutes of your time: prayer, personal care, sleep, meetings, eating, family time, sermon prep, reading, and so on. At the end of the week or month, total the hours on your log by category. How much time did you spend with your family? How much time did you spend sleeping, studying, attending meetings, counseling, and so on? How much time was spent on trivial activities, such as surfing the internet or watching videos? Identify the activities you feel are important and want to do yourself. How often do these important activities show up on your time log? Are you giving enough time to them? Why or why not? Commit to making these activities your priorities.

Identify time-wasting activities. Look at each activity you did during the last week or month and ask, "Which don't need to be done at all?" If they don't need to be done, stop doing them. Determine which of the activities can be done by someone else. These may include errands, attendance at meetings, counseling sessions, searching the web for sermon illustrations, and so on. Once you have your list, start asking others to do these activities for you. If you have a book to read, for example, ask a person in the church to read it for you, marking lines, paragraphs, or sections they think you should read. Ask them to search for possible sermon illustrations in the book too. When they return the book to you, just look at the places they've marked and resist reading the entire book. Does an item need to be picked up at the print shop? Ask someone to pick it up for you.

Ask yourself, "How have I wasted the time of others?" This is a tough question, but if you answer it honestly, you can prune the activities out of your own schedule, thereby making others around you more effective. One way that pastors waste time—theirs and that of others—is scheduling too many meetings. There are three problems with meetings: (1) meetings often accomplish little; (2) when people are meeting, ministry is not being done; and most problematic, (3) every meeting creates a need for more meetings—formal or informal. Some meetings are necessary, but there will always be more meetings than needed. One way to reduce meetings is to ask, "What is the agenda?" The rule: No agenda, no meeting. If the reason for meeting cannot be stated in a simple agenda, there is no need to meet.

Consolidate your time. Managing your time is really more about managing yourself. What most solo pastors learn by logging and analyzing their time usage is that they have about one-fourth of a workday—two hours maximum—to invest in important matters. The good news is you can do the important things if you consolidate your time into large chunks rather than trying to use small segments. Fifteen minutes here and there doesn't allow much of anything to be accomplished, but putting two hours together gives you a block of time when much can be completed.

When you first start setting boundaries on your time, you may find that you cut back too sharply. If this happens, don't worry. Others will let you know, and you can rebalance. Most solo pastors are unbalanced in doing too much rather than too little. As a solo pastor, you have more control over your time than you might admit. If you try, you can remove time-wasting activities and become more fruitful along the way. Effective solo pastors find it helpful to schedule meetings on one or two days a week, perhaps Monday and Friday. They may set aside Wednesday and Thursday mornings for sermon preparation, and perhaps all day Tuesday to work on other important matters. Other pastors create space by working from home, a nearby coffee shop, or a local library.

All that said, you still must tackle secondary, or less important, activities. By consolidating your time into blocks, however, you'll be able to sharpen your use of time. As months go by, what often

> *We should let our priorities be determined by the future that lies ahead rather than by the history that lies behind.*
>
> —*Edward R. Dayton and Ted W. Engstrom*

happens is your schedule gets slowly eaten by new crises, meetings, and demands. Without constant vigilance, your time will drift from managed to wasted. It takes vigilance to remain balanced, but it's worth doing.

3. Build a staff.

To be fruitful as a solo pastor, you must stop doing ministry by yourself and transition to helping others do ministry. It's similar to a person who works at making, say, refrigerators in a factory. If they hope to rise through the ranks from supervisor to middle manager and eventually to company president, they must stop thinking of making refrigerators and start thinking about over-seeing the people who make refrigerators. A New Testament term, *overseer* (Acts 20:28; 1 Pet. 5:2), contains the idea of managing the work of others. The solo pastor must do ministry with and for people but must also guide and direct (oversee) the people to do ministry (Eph. 4:11–12). Some have called this challenge the whiplash syndrome. Solo pastors suffer whiplash as they are jerked back and forth between doing ministry and guiding others to do ministry. It's not easy, but to be fruitful, solo pastors must work at building a team to share the doing of ministry.

Solo pastors may not have paid staff, but they do have a staff. The average attendee gives two hours beyond worship attendance to volunteering. People who give three hours or more of volunteer service a week are unpaid staff. Begin to think of them as your staff, and it'll change your perspective.

Understand that every person has a special calling. Paul reminds us, "We are His workmanship, created in Christ Jesus for good works, which God prepared beforehand so that we would walk in them" (Eph. 2:10). While we're all called to the common calling of being disciples, God prepared a special calling or work for each person. Thus, each person is uniquely gifted to serve in the body.

This may feel risky at first, but begin by asking newcomers to take on some responsibility—anything within reason—by their fourth visit. This could be such activities as filling out name tags, making coffee, setting up chairs, putting out Bibles, singing on a praise team, reading Scripture during a service, distributing bulletins/programs, or a host of other things. What usually happens is that newcomers wait, maybe for one to three years, before they're asked to help. That's a recipe for lack of involvement because the church is teaching them to sit rather than serve. Every person needs to feel wanted, and it's through serving that newcomers can make friends and connect with others in the church. Of course, each person is different, so asking others to serve must be applied carefully. Asking some newcomers to serve may potentially drive them away, while others who desire to be needed will welcome the opportunity.

Track every person's involvement, no matter how small your church. Your vision needs to be big enough to excite commitment to reach the larger community but small enough to involve every single person. Getting people involved and tracking them is an instant screening process for future leadership development. It shows you whether people are dependable, teachable, and open to learning. You'll observe quickly the natural leaders who initiate fresh ideas and strategies. Guide them spiritually so they grow, mature, and begin to influence the rest of the people positively. As people demonstrate responsible behavior, gradually ask them to extend their service and training. Prayerfully discern their motives, and invest more in those who are growing. When you take the risk of involving others, you'll encounter some disappointment along the way. Just take it in stride.

There are many ways to encourage people to serve, but some that worked in the past won't work so well today. A half century ago, one could easily motivate people to serve by challenging them to greater commitment. When someone tells you the church needs greater commitment, you can bet they are from an older generation, or at least are a long-term Christian. The danger is they have become more concerned about commitment than community. This type of person is quite often found in solo-pastor churches.

A better way to motivate people to serve in solo-pastor churches is through love and compassion. When Jesus spoke to Peter following the resurrection (after Peter had failed him), he didn't ask Peter to rise to a new level of commitment. Instead, he asked Peter to "tend My lambs," "shepherd My sheep," and "tend My sheep" (John 21:15–17). Jesus's appeal to serve was built on compassion and community.

Thus, when using commitment to motivate, you might say, "Sally, I challenge you to raise your commitment this next year by leading your own small group." She may accept the challenge, but after doing her duty, she may not renew her commitment the second year. A better way to motivate Sally for the long term is to say, "Sally, I invite you to build a community group where your compassion and love for one another can thrive."

4. Equip others to care.

A short history of pastoral care is helpful to understand where we've come from and where we are today. Pastoral care was in the hands of all believers in the early church (AD 100–475). The numerous "one anothers" of Scripture attest to the involvement of all believers in caring for each other. During the medieval period (476–1500), the church gradually moved to separate ministry roles, resulting in a clerical view of ministry in which the pastor expounded the Scriptures and provided care for church members. A distinction between clergy and laity arose that was only partially corrected in the Reformation period (1501–1648). In the modern period (1649–1959), a dependency model of pastoral ministry took hold, whereby the pastor provided individual care and the people were grateful (or ungrateful) recipients. This dependency model was especially supported in North America and could be compared to country doctors who were on call to provide care twenty-four hours a day, often without pay. New thinking emerged in the 1960s and '70s as frustrated pastors desired to get out of the hospital of pastoral care (chaplain) and into the battlefield of ministry. Pastoral care transitioned into crisis care, while more general care was given back to the congregation. Since 1980, the pastor's role has changed from that of a frontline medic for wounded Christians to a behind-the-line trainer of medics.

As long as the congregation expects the solo pastor to provide primary care and the pastor is willing to stay in that role, the church will not thrive. Negative consequences include the following: (1) the quality and quantity of care are limited to the capacity of the pastor; (2) church growth is restricted due to the church's lack of ability to provide care for the souls of new people; (3) the pastor won't have time to carry out their role of equipping the saints for ministry (Eph. 4:11–12); (4) there will be an unhealthy dependency and codependency between the solo pastor and the church; and (5) pastors will damage themselves physically, spiritually, emotionally, and relationally.

Paul, writing to the Galatians, indicates that some burdens are to be jointly shared and other loads are one's personal responsibility. He expresses this using two different Greek nouns. In 6:2 he writes, "Bear one another's burdens [*baros*]" to indicate burdens that are jointly shared. In verse 5 he writes, "Each one will bear his own load [*phortion*]" to indicate an individual's load of personal responsibility. These are different types of burdens. All Christians, not simply pastors, are to jointly share one another's burdens while not dismissing each individual's personal responsibility. Solo pastors must set boundaries to separate the two rather than being caught up in carrying loads that rightly belong to others.

5. *Remain visible.*

A common expectation of solo pastors is that they are visible to the congregation. This shows up when people visit shut-ins who ask, "Where's the pastor?" It is observed when church leaders at a church work day comment, "I thought the pastor was going to be here." And it is raised during weekly luncheons when people ask, "Where were you?" Each of these situations highlights the desire of people to see their pastor.

Setting priorities and boundaries will naturally remove you from some contact with your people. You may feel you are visible and available, while others in the church do not. For the most part, members of the congregation judge your availability based on your visibility at public gatherings. You may speak with only a few, but many more will see you and feel as though they could talk to you if they needed to. Having a warm personality and welcoming smile communicates accessibility. Each pastor has their own personality, of course, but making eye contact with people in the congregation while preaching, remembering names, and speaking to heart issues all serve to make one visible while communicating accessibility.

So when setting priorities and boundaries, bear in mind that you still need to be visible to people. There are several ways to accomplish this without abandoning your priorities. Walk through the lobby of the church slowly. Speak to a few people, looking into their eyes, giving full attention to what they say. Greet people by name. Have short conversations with some. Others will be watching and feel you are accessible. Send text messages and use social media—Twitter, Instagram, and other platforms—to remain in contact with and visible to people in your church. Some older members may desire your physical presence more often, but younger attendees may desire your presence only when needed. As part of your priorities, make some room for counseling and pastoral care. The key here is to make *some* room. Unless this area of ministry is your calling, maintain your boundaries. Limit your counseling to one or two meetings. If you can't solve people's problems in that number of meetings, refer them to a specialist who can give them the extended time they need.

6. *Make your family special.*

Where you'll be twenty years from now is greatly determined by how you treat your spouse and children today. The pressure to leave your family for ministry is strong in a solo-pastor church. External expectations from your people and your own internal expectations will make you think working from early morning to late at night is necessary. It isn't! Take a lesson from one pastor: "I nearly lost my wife and family from working too much. Thankfully, I was able to woo her back, but the real change came from changing my schedule. No longer do I schedule any evening meetings. You heard me right. I want to stay married to the same woman for years to come, so now I only schedule early morning meetings. It's made a clear difference in my relationship with my family, and I recommend other solo pastors try changing their schedule too."

THREE QUESTIONS

1. What is your LPOV?
2. Where do you spend your time? Is your time invested in your strengths or weaknesses? What do you need to keep doing, give away to others, and stop doing completely?
3. Who in your church volunteers three or more hours a week? When was the last time you met with them? How can you make them your staff?

TWO IDEAS

1. Take time this week to write down your leadership point of view and then share it with your board, secretary, and congregation. Then align your work to your LPOV. If you don't take control of your time by setting priorities, someone else will—and then how you spend your time most likely won't be a good match for your LPOV.
2. Who in your church has the gift of love, compassion, care, or helps? Call them together and ask them to start caring for others in your church. Train them and set them free to take over the general pastoral care for your church while you do occasion care and emergency care.

ELEVEN

Conquer Fear

The brave man is not he who does not feel afraid, but he who conquers that fear.

—Nelson Mandela

Jim." Bill spoke in a lower voice than usual. "I . . . I don't really know how to say this, so I guess I'll just say it. It's something I haven't shared with anyone, not even my wife. For the last few months, I've experienced a lot of sleepless nights. I wake up literally shaking with anxiety, feeling frightened. The first time it happened I thought maybe I was having a heart attack or something. But the feelings subsided rather quickly. Lately they've been more pronounced. One time it felt like I couldn't breathe."

"That's unfortunate," Jim empathized. "Tell me more."

"Two Sundays ago, right in the midst of preaching, I had a mild panic attack. For a few moments I wasn't sure I could even finish my sermon. The congregation didn't seem to notice the extended pause in my sermon, but inside I was struggling to hold it together. I honestly feel like I've hit a wall, sort of reached my limit, I guess is a way of putting it. I'm fearful of what's going to be my future at Faith Church. I hate to admit it, but I'm just plain afraid."

"Thanks for sharing this, Bill. I realize it's difficult to admit you're afraid, but it's good to get it out in the open," Jim affirmed. "I'm sure your lack of good sleep is contributing to your sense of fear. The great football coach Vince Lombardi once said, 'Fatigue makes cowards of us all.' He was right. Years ago, after I'd been in my church seven years, I hit a wall. During that time my church had tripled in size. We'd experienced a failed merger with a sister church, completed an extensive remodeling of the church campus, started a Christian school, and gone through a mild split when a key family left the church. I managed to get through it all until I had three funerals in one week. The following week I experienced feelings similar to what you just described. I needed to sleep but found it nearly impossible to do so. After a rough night's sleep, I'd go to church, close my office door, and lie down on my couch and sleep."

"Did people at church know that?" Bill asked.

"They probably thought I was praying." Jim suppressed a laugh. "The reality was I was exhausted and mildly depressed. I'd helped others grieve the loss of the church members who'd recently died but had not taken the time to grieve myself. I needed to grieve not only the death of those members but also the loss of the family that left the church and the failed merger."

"So what happened?" Bill asked.

"I wish I could say I worked through it, but I didn't. It took about a year, but eventually I moved on to a new ministry. The odd thing was, after I'd been in the new ministry about six months, I

Don't let the fear of striking out hold you back.

—Babe Ruth

told my wife, 'If I'd had a sabbatical from the other church, I'd probably still be there.' I just needed space to rest, think, grieve, and dream anew."

"That's me 100 percent! The crazy thing is I'm not really afraid of failing but more scared of succeeding. I'm already overwhelmed as it is. What will happen if our vision succeeds? What then?"

YES, WHAT IF BILL'S DREAM succeeds? What then? His fears are widespread among those pastoring churches alone, but you'll find them stated by pastors in all churches. Solo pastors mention the following seven fears as the most difficult to manage.

1. Fear of failure.

Fear of failure may be the most common type of fear among solo pastors. At least it's the most talked about. Solo pastors are lightning rods for criticism. Everything, including failure, is placed at their feet. Such fear keeps solo pastors from attempting to lead a church forward. If they start something new and it doesn't work, they'll be seen as a failure. If the church doesn't show some growth, they'll be seen as a failure among their peers. Underneath this fear is often a persistent perfectionism. Pastors don't try implementing a new direction for their church because they can't bear to do anything unless it's perfect. The reality, though, is that one can't be successful or fruitful unless something is done. New ministry must be started, people must be loved, food must be served, counsel must be given, and on and on. Failure is guaranteed unless action is taken, yet fear of failure stops actions—actions that could be successful or fruitful in moving the church toward a healthier life. It's a vicious circle.

2. Fear of success.

This fear is a difficult one to see and assess. It's directly related to the fear of failure but is recognized less by the majority of pastors. Don't all solo pastors desire success? Well, yes and no. Pastors are prone to dismiss the idea of success, instead inserting the word *faithful*, as in, "I'm called to be faithful, not successful." Yet faithfulness implies success—success at being faithful. If God calls pastors to be faithful, and they are faithful, then aren't they successful? Unfortunately, solo pastors undermine themselves in subtle ways that keep them from success. Here are a few examples of how this happens. A pastor has the opportunity to challenge a church bully but doesn't do it. A pastor finds the church willing to start a new ministry but doesn't follow through. The congregation is waiting for the pastor to communicate a new vision for the future, but it's never done. Why? Perhaps the pastor is scared of what might happen if they succeed. What happens if the bully backs down? What happens if the new ministry works? What happens if the congregation buys in to the new vision? If the new measures succeed, then what?

3. Fear of discovery.

This shows up in almost every field of work. It even has its own name: impostor syndrome. Professors, for example, are fearful that other professors are going to discover they're not as good at their craft as they appear. Pastors fear people will find out they're not as strong in prayer or evangelism or as deeply spiritual as they may appear. This is the fear of being found out. This fear stops pastors from preaching well. They stop short of revealing their own struggles in ways that would make them more appealing to parishioners who are struggling with their own issues of life. It stops them from disciple-making because they fear getting close to others who will see them for who they really are. It stops them from taking others along on hospital visitations because others will find out they're not good at providing care.

4. Fear of not measuring up.

Some have called the congregational setting "one of the most dangerous of all for people given to overcommitment."[1] Solo pastors are by nature, of course, susceptible to overcommitment. The churches they serve take advantage of them, sometimes run them into the ground, due to this trait. The problem is exacerbated by the fact that pastors put unreasonable (unbearable?) expectations on themselves. How does one measure up to unreasonable expectations? One doesn't. When a solo pastor expects too much of themselves, they are headed for an emotional, mental, spiritual, and physical breakdown that shows itself in the fear of not measuring up to expectations.

5. *Fear of comparison.*

One pastor commented, "I'm supposed to stand up in a pulpit and hold people's attention, be as articulate as the best preacher on television, and be as good-looking as the top media personality. I hate the comparisons." Such comparisons even go so far as comparing the size of one church to another. God never promised any pastor a big church. He did promise that his church would grow (Matt. 16:18), but that doesn't automatically translate into a single church growing larger. Nevertheless, solo pastors admit to a great fear of being compared to the pastors of larger churches. Protecting their self-image and reputation is paramount for some. Comparison with pastors serving locally or even those found on the internet is devastating to them. Any mention of another pastor's preaching ability, the available programs in other churches,

> *Inaction breeds doubt and fear. Action breeds confidence and courage. If you want to conquer fear, do not sit home and think about it. Go out and get busy.*
>
> —*Dale Carnegie*

or the dynamic worship found in another church brings feelings of disgust or envy. When their feelings seep out in meetings or while preaching, they may be viewed by those listening as angry and bitter, neither of which is good.

6. Fear of not doing enough.

The solo pastor never hears, "Hey, the job is done." There's always more to do in a solo-pastor church. The sermon may be finished, but next Sunday's coming. Workers have been recruited for the children's ministry, but more will be needed next fall. Finances squeaked into the black this year, but next year's going to be more challenging. Ministry flows to the pastor like water out of a fire hydrant—fast and forceful. Pastors question whether they've ever done enough, whether ministry demands will ever stop no matter how hard they work. The solo pastor's job is never completely finished. When will enough be enough? Face it: ministry can be like a narcotic—an escape from a bad marriage, a painful past, or broken dreams. By doing more and more, you're robbing yourself of vital things—most often connection to family and friends. And you never even realize it until you go to look for them and find they're gone.

7. Fear of loss.

One solo pastor said, "Pastoring a church is a constant struggle with feelings of loss." The losses are easy to enumerate: loss of friends, loss of financial supporters, loss of gifted workers, loss of visionaries, loss of hope, and what may be the most difficult, loss of a dream. A pastor recently related how he needed to confront the worship leader of his church, but it was his best friend. He knew that after the confrontation his friend would leave the church. This fear of losing a close friend stopped him for many months from doing what needed to be done. The resulting turmoil affected the entire congregation and subsided only after he finally spoke with his friend. His friend did leave the church, confirming the pastor's fear.

GETTING FREE OF THESE seven fears begins with recognizing that the one you serve is God, not the church members, your peers, or others who may be watching. Solo pastors are servants of God first, before serving others. The words of the writer of Hebrews offer encouragement: "Let us run with endurance the race that is set before us, fixing our eyes on Jesus, the author and perfecter of faith" (12:1–2). No one faced as much potential fear as Jesus did. He faced tremendous pressures that could have driven him into nervous states of fear, but he stood strong in the face of opposition. As he faced fears, so can you. Here are some tips to help you redeem fears for fruitful ministry.

1. Invest in your own leadership development.

"No one ever told me, nor did I ever read, how difficult it'd be to lead myself," declared a discouraged pastor. It's axiomatic that if you can't lead yourself, you can't lead others. Start with asking God to transform you. Read books, interview effective pastors, take classes on leadership, and lead your own church right now. Start where you are and notch up your skills a little every year. In five years, you'll be five years older no matter what you do. By investing in yourself today, you'll be better in five years. While leadership isn't about you, it always starts with you.

Focus on your strengths more than your weaknesses. Self-acceptance doesn't come easy to solo pastors. The tendency is to work on your weaknesses. One pastor quipped, "You may teach a dog to ride a horse, but he'll never win a rodeo." You may improve your weaknesses, but you'll never be as good in your weaknesses as you are in your strengths. As a solo pastor, you must work on your weaknesses, but it's best to recognize your strengths and stick with them as much as reasonable. Think of your gifts, talents, and abilities in three categories: A, B, and C. A is where you excel. B is what you do okay but don't excel at. C is what you struggle to do at all. Give yourself permission to work primarily in the A category, perhaps 70 percent of the time. Give category B maybe 25 percent of the time, while C gets 5 percent. This is just conceptual, as each pastor must work within a specific church environment. The idea is to focus on your strengths. What do you do with your weaknesses? You find others who excel in the areas you don't and give that part of ministry to them.

2. Practice biblical humility.

Humility is not self-doubt or false modesty. It's being clear about your own strengths and weaknesses while understanding that you need others to help you succeed. Do what you can to bless others. Don't fear gifted people in your church. Bless them by drawing them into ministry with you. Don't criticize pastors of larger churches. Bless them, remembering that you'll both stand before God to account for your own labors.

There is no need to fear being compared with other pastors. God has given them their field and flock, and he's given you yours. Peter commands pastors to "shepherd the flock of God among you" (1 Pet. 5:2). The phrase "among you" is difficult to translate, but the phrase that follows, "exercising oversight," clears up the meaning. You cannot exercise oversight of a flock that is not yours. Thus, a pastor's job is to take care of the flock God has given them. Don't worry about another pastor's flock. Just take care of your own.

3. Reject worm theology.

The Bible speaks a great deal about the human condition. Some of it is bad—we've all sinned (Rom. 3:23)—and some of it is good—we all are gifted (1 Pet. 4:10). Solo pastors (perhaps all pastors) find it easy to accept the bad but struggle to accept the good. Feeling that God doesn't want us to succeed is worm theology. David did declare, "I am a worm and not a man" (Ps. 22:6), but he was crying out in anguish as others attacked him. He wasn't talking about his standing before God. In Psalm 23, David speaks of God's blessing on his life. His cup overflows, and goodness and mercy will follow him all the days of his life. In practice, some pastors picture themselves as losers (worms) rather than winners (blessed of God), or at least they find it difficult to believe they can be successful. How often have you heard someone excuse their lack of fruitfulness with the statement "God doesn't require us to be successful, only faithful"? There is biblical merit behind such a statement, but perhaps it's used too frequently to excuse self-defeating behavior.

Worm theology comes from an incorrect concept of God and how he works. The principle of cause and effect was established by God, and right results normally come from right actions. The loving heavenly Father wants you to succeed, when your success comes in the right way, with the right motive, while sharing in his work. A biblical definition of success says, "Success is reaching the master's goals with the gifts he has given us."[2] You are a success if you make the most of your potential. If you measure your success by how you're using the gifts God has given you, you will eliminate much frustration. You may have limited opportunities and resources, but using what you have to fulfill God's call on your life is success. Don't set up artificial boundaries. Stop working not to lose. Don't serve just to hold on to your job. God gives you permission to succeed. Work to succeed, to faithfully guide your church into a better future.

4. Do the basics.

If you've ever played organized sports, you know that there are basics that form the foundation of all good play. The same is true in pastoral ministry. The basics form a foundation for fruitful work. The basics of pastoral ministry remain the same: preach, teach, lead, care, oversee, love, and so on. Doing the basics well provides courage to innovate, move toward a new future, and tackle more difficult items. Stay focused on doing the basics while you try to solve more complex issues. One pastor puts it this way: "You'll never solve the complex problems facing your leadership by ignoring the basic responsibilities of your leadership."[3] You will have to

> *The only thing we have to fear is fear itself.*
> —*Franklin D. Roosevelt*

pay the rent by doing the basics, but make sure people also know you're committed to working out Ephesians 4:11–12 by equipping them for service. Ultimately, your credibility has less to do with your performance and more to do with your steady faithfulness in difficult situations. As you demonstrate a pattern of consistently doing your job, fear will be removed. It's always wise to recall, however, that your job is not to please people. "Just as we have been approved by God to be entrusted with the gospel, so we speak, not as pleasing men, but God who examines our hearts" (1 Thess. 2:4).

5. *Maximize your leadership.*

Churches need strong leadership. In fact, the decline of churches indicates they aren't being led very well. The problem is twofold. On one side, there are people who try to bridle pastors and keep them under control. Driven by fear, some churches set up internal structures that stop the pastor from leading. On the other side, pastors fail to step forward to provide directive leadership. Driven by fear, they recoil from leading as they ought. Sadly, both sides add to the creation of anemic leadership. The apostle Paul combats leadership fears by challenging leaders to lead with "diligence" (Rom. 12:8). Another way to put this might be, "Leaders, get going. Lead with haste and zeal."

6. *Get in the back of the boat.*

Right before Jesus calmed the storm (Mark 4:35–41), he was in the back of the boat—sleeping. It's a part of the story that is often missed, but Jesus wasn't preaching, teaching, or healing. He was sleeping! He needed the break from ministering to others. Like him, solo pastors need a break from ministry activities. They need to take a break to remember why they're in ministry, whom they serve, and that they are valuable for who they are, not just what they do. Learn what fuels your ministry passion. If it's love, gratitude, obedience, and mercy, you're on good ground, but if it's pride, envy, people pleasing, or proving yourself worthy, you're on shaky ground. Practicing gratitude for what you already have—ministry, influence, family—alleviates fear as you recognize that God is renewing your strength day by day.

7. Move at a "savoring pace."

Pastor Kirk B. Jones writes, "Jesus did not hurry into action" when he calmed the sea (Mark 4:35–41); rather, he moved at a "savoring pace" that is "characterized by peace, patience, and attentiveness."[4] Moving at a savoring pace involves, among other things, intentionally slowing down at some points, saying no to things more often, and practicing stillness (a quiet delight of being yourself and being with God). Jones recommends stepping into the back of the boat each morning by sipping your morning BREW:

- Be still.
- Receive God's love.
- Embrace God's gift of personhood.
- Welcome the day and its opportunities to offer and receive blessings.[5]

YOU CAN'T LEAD others if you're not in the game yourself, so stay in the game! Fear may point you to the sidelines, but it's impossible to grow and overcome fear sitting on the bench. Overcoming the many fears in ministry comes from having enough courage to get in the game. Ask God to give you the courage to do what you need to do. "For God gave us a spirit not of fear but of power and love and self-control" (2 Tim. 1:7 ESV).

— THREE QUESTIONS —

1. What fears noted in this chapter do you see popping up in your own life?
2. Are you able to redeem your fears for good? If so, what practices help you do so? If not, what keeps you from doing so?
3. Which of the ideas for redeeming your fears are most helpful to you? Why?

— TWO IDEAS —

1. Meet with two or three pastors and ask them what fears they face in ministry. Share stories and ways you've found to overcome the fears.
2. Pick two of the ideas mentioned and start putting them into practice this week. If you have other ideas that may help you face your fears, list them here. Which ones will you put into practice this week?

TWELVE

Redeem Stress

You take care of you for me, and I will take care of me for you.

—Jim Rohn

There's still one thing I haven't brought up that I'd like to discuss with you, Jim."

"I'm game," Jim responded with enthusiasm.

"I'll describe it this way. A few years ago, I took my children to an air show at our local air force base. One of the events was a flyby of jet planes in formation, where one of the planes was flying upside down. For some reason, that image reminds me of being a pastor—that is, flying an airplane upside down. It's a big adrenaline rush and fun most of the time. But there's always an aching feeling that I'm all alone in the cockpit, sort of a loneliness."

"Bill, I've felt that way numerous times. It's often said, as you know, that it's lonely at the top."

"I've heard that before, but I always believed it was overstated. Now that I'm a solo pastor, I find it's true—I'm lonely. But it's not all about being lonely. It's the stress of leading and managing ministry. Sometimes I fantasize about having a staff, at least a small one. In my mind, I think I'd get a lot more done, but I'm not sure I would. I guess what I really want is someone to share the stress or burden of ministry."

"Bill, I've found that sometimes we pastors define ourselves through our problems—like being lonely—when what we really need is a friend. What we're really trying to do is get people to notice us and our needs."

"I can see that," Bill added. "I'm so busy helping others that I wonder who's concerned about me. The honest truth is I'm tired. It seems like I'm never at home, constantly on call, working way more hours than anyone should. Added to that, here I am, trained in Bible and theology, but I'm expected to manage conflict, master leadership, understand finance, and manage all the activities of a church. It's all stressful. And, of course, I have to do all this by myself—alone."

"Have you talked with your wife about your feelings?"

"Of course, but it's to the point that I can't talk to her any longer about it. She can only take so much of my discouragement, Jim."

"Man, I didn't realize you were so discouraged, Bill. Let me ask this: How's your prayer life?"

"I try to pray, but my prayer life isn't as strong as it was when I first came to Faith Church. The first year I was here, I made it a priority to get on my knees by my desk at 9 a.m. and pray for thirty minutes every day. Somewhere, somehow—I don't really know when or why—I stopped doing it. Now it's a struggle to pray. Jim, I hate to say this, but most days I just want to quit. I really don't know where to turn."

REPORTS CIRCULATE CONSTANTLY on the internet and among pastors about large numbers of pastors quitting each month due to loneliness, physical burnout, moral failure, and internal strife in their churches. Such reports are overstated, and controlled studies (versus rumor) point out that turnover among pastors is about the same as for other stressful jobs.[1] Nonetheless, most pastors do work long hours, sacrifice time with family to care for their congregations, and feel lonely—particularly solo pastors. It's strange, but loneliness is commonly found in people who have numerous social connections, like pastors. Because so much of a pastor's time is spent alone in prayer and study, it can lead to feelings of isolation and a lack of close connections. With so much time inside their own minds, pastors feel they face ministry—and the world—alone, even with numerous social connections in the church. When asked if they have a close friend, as high as 70 percent of solo pastors reported they have no close friend.[2] No wonder solo pastors are lonely. God has designed us to be nourished by relationships, and pastors who feel lonely have a higher risk of addiction, suicide, hypertension, impaired immunity, heart attack, stroke, and illness.

Loneliness, however, is just one expression of even deeper issues. Loneliness is often a symptom of stress. Stress is an ongoing feeling of never catching up. Solo pastors regularly feel there are too many things to do and they're never going to catch up. Initial symptoms of stress are physical: headaches, backaches, reduced energy, weight gain, high blood pressure, irritability, a loss of drive, and insomnia. Over time, emotional and spiritual symptoms surface: depression, guilt, anxiety, disillusionment, discouragement, and loneliness. When we encounter pain, it's usually a signal that something is wrong. For instance, hunger pains let us know it's time to eat, knee pain alerts us to possible injury, and loneliness points to potential spiritual, emotional, and physical vulnerability.

So, what must a solo pastor do to bring spiritual, emotional, and physical balance back to their life? Essentially, they return to what is vital to revitalize. The following are practical steps, listed in no particular order, that can be redemptive for solo pastors.

1. Secure your own oxygen mask.

If you've ever flown, you'll recall the flight attendant announcing various instructions prior to takeoff. One announcement that seems illogical is to "secure your own oxygen mask before helping others." At first thought, this sounds rather selfish. Wouldn't it be best to help others first and think of yourself last? On second thought, however, it's clear that securing your own mask first is crucial. If you can't breathe, you won't be able to help anyone else.

In many cases, solo pastors run around helping others secure their masks (requests, errands, visits, calls, etc.) while neglecting to put on their own masks (personal rest, exercise, eating right). Eventually they run out of oxygen, becoming mentally, spiritually, emotionally, and physically unhealthy.

Overall, the most satisfied solo pastors are those who are methodical about taking care of themselves. As the old saying goes, "You can't pour water from an empty cup."

2. Gather with other pastors in your community.

As a solo pastor, you won't be able to be as open, authentic, and vulnerable as you'd like at church. Then, too, you can share only so much with your spouse, and they can take only so much.

> *Most pastors will admit, when asked about their personal and professional lives, that serving God in a church often also means loneliness, lack of opportunities for ongoing professional and personal development, and external and internal pressure to overlook one's own health in the service of others.*
>
> *—Jackson Carroll*

Find other pastors who can be real with you. Rest assured, other pastors are overtaxed and aching for someone to share their burdens with too.

At first you may need an agenda, such as helping each other prepare for preaching. Be ready to stop and just talk to each other. Issues will come up—criticism from people, a church fight, a problem to solve. When they do, stop, talk, and pray with each other. You'll be surprised how effective such a group is at alleviating feelings of stress.

Gathering with a safe, open, transparent group of peers is an excellent way to end the isolation that naturally comes with solo pastoring. Unfortunately, some communities of pastors struggle with competition, with each pastor trying to outdo the others with stories of ministry success. Other groups end up as negative gripe sessions. Neither is helpful. If a healthy group already exists, join it. If you can't find one, start one. Ask other pastors in your community to gather each month. The connections you make will be life-giving for you and the others too.

3. Have a life outside your church.

When solo pastors think about what they do outside the church, the usual answer is nothing. Church ministry consumes their lives as well as the lives of their family members because it's all the pastors are engaged in. This makes everything that happens in the church larger than it often is. Everything that takes place at church has a greater impact than it would if church ministry was just one aspect of a fuller life.

Solo pastors have the mistaken idea that if their church is healthy, they'll be healthy too. The endless running about to cater to the needs of the church is done in hopes of helping it become healthy, but it often has the opposite effect. The reality is if the pastor is healthy, the church can be healthy.

One way to ensure your health as a pastor is to have a life outside the church. Do things that energize you. Put some fun back in your life. Find a hobby, play a sport, walk in the woods (or on a beach or around the neighborhood), visit museums—do things besides attend church meetings and activities. One pastor wrote, "I enrolled in a class on woodworking. It was wonderful. I found it so invigorating to stand back and look at a finished table, for example, and see that it was done. Ministry always has an incomplete feel about it. Woodworking was just the opposite. The table was done. Done! It was tight, square, plumb. Such a great feeling." Woodworking may not be for you, but find something—golfing, motorcycling, reading, listening to music, skiing, flying a plane (or a kite), taking a long bath or shower—unrelated to ministry that will allow you space to recharge your depleted emotional, spiritual, and physical batteries.

4. Take a Sabbath rest each week, quarter, and year.

Being a solo pastor is challenging. The high expectations, along with potential work outside the church, make it tiring. At minimum, take one day off each week to refresh your mind and soul. And certainly take a yearly vacation of two weeks in succession. But days off and vacations are not enough. You also need a regular time to let your solo-pastor brain relax. One way to do this that won't infringe on church ministry is to take one weekend a quarter off. A glance at a calendar reveals there are thirteen weeks in every quarter of the year. Ask your church board to grant you the thirteenth weekend off. Cost to the church will be minimal, even if they need to pay a speaker to take those four Sundays a year. The benefits for giving you time to rest, pray, think, or sleep will be multiplied in better ministry the other twelve weeks.

Taking a sabbatical is another way to get some rest, and even help your church. Before starting a new ministry, discuss your expectations for a sabbatical. Explain the need for and the positive outcomes of granting a leave after a certain number of years of service. Assuming the church grants a sabbatical, write it into your terms of call, placement, or contract. If they don't grant you a sabbatical, bring it up again in a few years, as the leaders may rotate or change their minds. You can also do a stay-batical, which is sort of like a stay-cation, where families vacation by going to venues close to their home. A stay-batical happens by setting and following strict boundaries between work and home life, reducing the number of meetings and appointments, maintaining tighter work hours, and getting away for short sabbaticals—say, every Tuesday morning from 8 a.m. to noon or the first Friday of every month, during which you go out of town for rest and recuperation.

If the church feels it can't grant a sabbatical due to the financial cost, consider a do-it-yourself sabbatical. One pastor shared a plan he followed to take three one-year sabbaticals in a twenty-year stint as a solo pastor. Over the course of six years, he saved one-sixth of his salary each year. He then took a full-year sabbatical in the seventh year and paid for it himself by drawing down the savings. During the year he was off, the church used the money they normally paid him for a salary to make necessary repairs and updates and to build up its own savings for future emergencies. Prior to his sabbatical year, the pastor worked with four elders to develop twelve sermons each. They then took turns preaching once each month for the year he was away and invited in only four guest speakers to cover the thirteenth Sunday of each quarter. Not only did this plan give him extended rest, but his elders also grew and discovered how difficult it is to be a solo pastor.

5. Have friendships outside the church.

Leaders in all fields of work struggle with feelings of loneliness, but solo pastors are most at risk. Some people find it easy to make friends, but others don't. For younger families, friends are easily made through children's activities, such as youth sports. Parents gather to watch their children practice and play games and often go out for refreshments afterward. This is an opportunity to meet others and develop friendships. Making friends gets more difficult as one grows older, since children are no longer around to engender friendships among parents. As a general rule, the younger you are, the more friends you have, but the friendships are not deep. The older you are, the fewer friends you have, but the friendships have depth. Either way, it's important to figure out a way to connect with people for one's own health. Friends can be found where people volunteer and serve, such as food banks, museums, clothing recycling centers, and the like. In most cases friends won't come to you easily, so you'll have to find them wherever possible.

Making friends with nonchurched people can be one of the best ways to refresh your life. Getting to know people who don't attend church opens new lines of communication, understanding, and passion for ministry. When you have friends who are lost without Christ, you have a renewed compassion. You see afresh the hopelessness and self-destructiveness of life apart from Christ. Your desire for evangelism grows stronger.

Once you've made new friends, try not to skim along the surface with them. Skimming offers the bare minimum connection, without much depth. Think of a water-skier skimming along on the surface of a lake. Their skis rarely get low into the water. Skimming is good for waterskiing but not for friendship. When you are with your friends, be there. One pastor put it this way: "Building friendships is about being who you are, where you are, when you are, with whom you are." When you're with friends, focus on them—their lives, careers, families, interests, and needs. By doing so, your friendships will grow deeper, and they'll be there for you when you need them too.

6. Get adequate rest and exercise, and eat right.

As a group, pastors are less physically fit and face more frequent exhaustion than the average person.[3] Psalm 127:1–2 is instructive: "Unless the LORD builds the house, they labor in vain who build it; unless the LORD guards the city, the watchman keeps awake in vain. It is vain for you to rise up early, to retire late, to eat the bread of painful labors; for He gives to His beloved even in his sleep." This passage sounds like it was written directly to solo pastors. For most, it is vain to retire late, rise early, and eat the bread of painful labors. A seasoned pastor put it this way: "I'm an early riser, so from 5:30 in the morning until I crash at 10:30 at night, there's barely a moment that is not related to something at church. I don't work out at the YMCA any longer. When I ride my bike, I listen to CDs to find sermon illustrations. I'm always on church time." Without the Lord's involvement, work—even extra hard, long days—is vain. The psalm says that God gives to his beloved in his sleep. God is gracious in giving solo pastors good things even during their sleep. And sleep is refreshing by itself.

One of the most spiritual things you can do as a solo pastor is to go to bed. Solo pastors end their days mentally, emotionally, spiritually, and physically exhausted. The tendency is to work late to make up for lost time during the day. It's better, however, to go to bed earlier and get up an hour earlier the next morning. Rest restores, as the psalmist knows, and God's mercies are new every morning (Lam. 3:21–23).

Finding and establishing a rhythm for your life is crucial. God set the example by creating the world in six days, after which he rested. Rested! He could have finished the creation sooner, and he didn't need to rest, but he set a pattern, a rhythm, for life and work. Each day when the work was done, he called it a day. As a pastor, you need to "call it a day" and celebrate what you've accomplished—it is good.

Too much sleep is not good, however. Salt is good, but too much is unhealthy. Going to the gym or investing in some other physical activity is good too. You need a healthy body to lead a healthy church. Numerous studies link healthy eating and exercise to reduced stress. The dangers are the more we need them, the less we think we need them. Solo pastors end up eating too much fast food, while drinking too many sugary drinks or coffee loaded with unhealthy creamers. Like any investment, exercise has to be scheduled and allowed to build up over time. If you don't exercise, rest, and eat properly, you'll end up giving God only two-thirds of your potential energy. Committing yourself to the physical disciplines of running, weight lifting, stretching, or other activities will assist you in offering yourself wholly to God in mind, spirit, and body.

7. Revitalize your spiritual life.

Jesus said, "Come to Me, all who are weary and heavy-laden, and I will give you rest. Take My yoke upon you and learn from Me, for I am gentle and humble in heart, and you will find rest for your souls. For My yoke is easy and My burden is light" (Matt. 11:28–30). Most pastors wake up drained on Monday mornings. The intense ministry activities engaged in on Sunday leave them worn down. Recharging emotional energy takes more than just a few minutes. Similar to recharging a car battery, it's best to use a slow, consistent charge to bring back your emotional energy after it's been drained. To do this, you don't always need to take several months off (see #4 above). There are other ways to breathe fresh life into your soul. Spending more time in prayer is a key aspect of revitalizing your spiritual energy. In contrast to loneliness, silence and solitude is an intentional time of isolation from social connection that can increase concentration, creativity, and productivity. It provides time for reflection and to think about God's Word. It also gives you time to reflect on the fact that you are not alone in ministry. Jesus promises that he will never leave or forsake you. As Jesus told his disciples, "I am with you always, even to the end of the age" (Matt. 28:20). Practice other spiritual disciplines such as Bible reading, fasting, or journaling. Writing out prayers is a superb way to unleash your spiritual energy and propel you back into the loving arms of Jesus. If you find it helpful to type your thoughts on a computer, tablet, or phone, that's okay, but using a stylus or writing out your words on paper makes you process your thoughts and feelings into words.[4]

Signs of Loneliness

· Being overwhelmed with isolation
· Being unable to connect deeply with others
· Being exhausted after trying to connect with others
· Being disillusioned about one's abilities
· Being unseen and unheard
· Being without a close friend

---

8. Get back to using your major gifts—again!

The multiple demands on a solo pastor slowly pull them away from the work they most enjoy. One way to restore energy and redeem stress is to start using one's major spiritual gifts again. Using one's gifts restores focus, delight, and affirmation from God. In most situations, you'll feel more energized after using your primary gifts.

9. Keep your feet on the ground.

It's unwise to daydream in the clouds of maybes and might-have-beens. Find practical ways to bring yourself back to earth. Find a few church assessment and evaluation tools to administer in your church in order to determine what's really happening. One way to do this is to track what's happened in your church over the last few years. List what's important for your church to evaluate. Most churches find it helpful to monitor the number of people involved in small groups or classes, the number of baptisms each year, the number of people serving others in ministry, and, yes, church attendance (in person, online, etc.). Tracking such things helps you see what is really happening, and while it doesn't tell you what to do, it does take away any illusions you might have. You might discover the church is doing better than you thought and your worries are unfounded. Or perhaps the church is doing worse and you can take action. Either way, it's better to know the facts than to simply dwell in the fog.

Another way to assess your church is to list the stories of people who are being discipled, new or renewed faith in God, redeemed lives, service to others, and so on. Looking at such stories moves you from focusing on just the negatives to seeing the positive happenings at your church. Express gratitude daily for what God is doing in and through your church. Write down the good things God is doing, and read your list before you turn in for the night. Maybe this is part of the reason the apostle Paul encourages solo pastors (and all believers), "Whatever is true, whatever is honorable, whatever is right, whatever is pure, whatever is lovely, whatever is of good repute, if there is any excellence and if anything worthy of praise, dwell on these things" (Phil. 4:8). It's deadly to wish things will get better rather than appreciating the good things already taking place. By pondering and thinking about these things habitually, not only will you sleep better and be less stressed, but you'll also wake up more refreshed. It's a simple practice that more solo pastors need to do.

10. Find a mentor.

You want someone who will lift you up when you're down and take you down a notch when needed. Ideally, this person is older and more experienced than you, someone who is ahead of you in ministry and can empathize with you, someone who understands what you're going through, someone who can offer advice, wisdom, and maybe even a hug or two.

The person you want to mentor you is likely not looking for you. They are probably busy and not looking to schedule another meeting, so you'll need to find them. Step up and courageously ask them to meet with you. Volunteer to pay for their help, or at least for dinner. Come to the meeting prepared with one or two key questions and then listen. Listen! This is a time to ask questions and learn rather than vent your own issues. Remember: a mentor offers you guidance, not answers.

11. *Put down your phone.*

There's an ongoing debate as to whether a person can be addicted to digital media. Whether or not you believe you're addicted to your phone, you probably realize it keeps you from connecting well with others—at least when you are face-to-face eating a meal, for instance. Think it doesn't affect you? Take this short, admittedly unscientific, quiz.

How many days this week have you . . .

_____ checked your cell phone before getting out of bed?

_____ had five minutes of internet activity turn into thirty or more minutes?

_____ monitored your cell phone in the bathroom?

_____ checked your phone while talking with others (even just a peek)?

_____ texted while walking?

_____ texted while driving (be honest, I won't tell)?

_____ picked up your cell phone just for comfort (it feels nice in your hand)?

_____ walked into something (door, chair, dog, someone else) while on your phone?

_____ ignored or stopped listening to another person while on your phone?

_____ said, "Just a moment, I need to check Twitter/ Facebook/Instagram"?

_____ TOTAL

If your total is

0–15: You likely have many friends.

16–30: Others may feel ignored when around you.

31–45: Others definitely feel ignored when around you.

46+: I'm not saying you're lonely, but . . .

Jesus spent time with people where they worked and lived. His teaching showed his acquaintance with people's lives: a sower going out to sow, a woman sweeping her floor, a man settling his accounts, a shepherd tending sheep. These are the stories of a man who was connected with others. To aid in removing feelings of loneliness and redeeming stress, consider turning off your cell phone whenever you're around people. Take part in conversations completely free of any digital interruptions. The next time your laptop, tablet, or phone runs out of power, stop using it for the rest of the day. Talk with people face-to-face instead. Cell phones, computers, and tablets are all wonderful tools for ministry, but they also isolate us in our own lonely worlds.

SOLO PASTORS ARE God's "workmanship, created in Christ Jesus for good works" (Eph. 2:10). Note, however, that the workman comes before the good works. Being a solo pastor can be a stressful and lonely job, but it's not just a job. It's an amazing and difficult calling. While your church should seek to care for you, you must also take responsibility to exercise self-care. You must take care to develop friendships, get rest, spend time exercising, and [insert your own self-care need here]. Investing in your own health will reduce loneliness and stress while creating the opportunity to lead a heathier church.

THREE QUESTIONS

1. If nothing changes, how long do you have before you burn out?
2. Are you working from your primary gifting and strengths? When do you say, "I love doing this"? What gifts are you using as you say it?

3. What activities outside church can you enjoy and have a chance to be with your family? Schedule some of these activities on your next day off or for your next vacation.

TWO IDEAS

1. Ask a small group of wise and godly people to pray for you weekly and give you feedback on how you're coming across to others. Listen to them and follow their advice.

2. List two of your gifts (strengths) and two areas where you're not gifted (limitations). For one month, focus on working from your gifts while limiting the work that really isn't in you. After one month, assess your fruitfulness and go from there.

Take Flight

A pastor ought to be something, ought to know something, and ought to do something.

—John A. Broadus

I had no idea how draining, how frustrating ministry really is. No one told me how much I'd struggle with all the demands on my time and how difficult it would be to simply take care of myself," Bill recalled. "I want you to know how valuable our conversations have been over the last few months."

"Yep, I know what you mean." Jim confirmed Bill's thoughts. "No one ever told me what it was like to be a solo pastor either. I have to admit that much of what you're feeling I've felt too. There were times when I almost quit. Have you had similar feelings?"

Bill sighed. "Yes, I hate to say it out loud, but I've dreamed of quitting. Many times when I'm in my office alone, I'll drift into daydreaming about how I wish my church would be better. It lets me escape from the realities I'm facing. I know it doesn't help matters, but I fantasize what Jesus's ideal church might look like. In my mind I compare my fictional ideal church to the real church I pastor, and it causes me to think about quitting."

"The fact is," Jim interjected, "Jesus dwells in your church as it actually exists."

"I know. I know that, at least in my mind," Bill acknowledged. "So, where do I go from here?"

"I remember reading a story about a decade ago," Jim began. "Let me tell you the story as I recall it. An older pastor shared that one day he had two unexpected, painful encounters. The first took place when he visited a family from his church. When he got to the house, the family's youngest child, a girl about five years old, saw him and ran up to the door of the house and shouted, 'Mommy, Mommy, the angry man who shouts in church is here.' Her words shocked the pastor. Later that same day, the pastor met an elderly couple at church. He began sharing excitedly about the church's new building project when the older man interrupted him, saying, 'I sometimes wonder if there's a quiet part in you.' Caught off guard, the pastor asked, 'Quiet part? What do you mean?' to which the older man replied, 'Every time we see you, you're all wound up, talking about projects and programs. You speak about Jesus only in sermons, never in conversations. We're up in years, and we'd like to know that our pastor has a quiet side where Jesus whispers in his life for the benefit of others.' The pastor commented that heaven spoke to him that day through those two encounters. He began to ask himself, 'What kind of leader am I becoming: a peaceful leader who connects with others or an organizational leader who uses them?' That's a good question to ponder. Don't you agree?"[1]

"Offhand, I'd say I want to be a peaceful leader, but I still want the church to move forward."

"Of course the church should move forward," Jim admitted. "I've found that ultimately you have to get into God's Word. My suggestion is that you look at Nehemiah. It might be a game changer for you."

"How so?" Bill asked.

"Nehemiah has a lot to say about leading a church. He experienced opposition and had many of the same feelings that we have, such as fear, loneliness, disappointment, weariness, desperation— you name it. Yet he experienced much success, or fruit, if you prefer that term. He never quit, and God blessed him and his work as he faithfully served God's purpose."

"Sounds like I need to go back and study Nehemiah again," Bill assented.

"One more story," Jim said. "I'm not sure if it's true, but I heard an old story that goes something like this. Years ago, there was a man who loved soda. Eventually he decided to go into the soda business himself. He called his first product 3UP, but people didn't like it, and it failed. So he reformulated it and tried again, naming it 4UP. Unfortunately, even though he worked hard to make it a success, it failed too. Not being one to give up, he hired some chemists to help develop a new formula and tried again, naming it 5UP. Sure enough, it failed again. He told his chemists to get back to work on an entirely new formula, while he turned his attention to marketing the new soda, now named 6UP. It too failed. He was completely discouraged but decided to give it one more try. This time he named the drink 7UP, which became a huge success. The story is likely apocryphal, but it does teach a lesson."

"You're telling me not to give up," Bill asserted.

"That's what I'm saying. Spiritual leadership is never easy, particularly as a solo pastor. But that's no reason to quit."

"Okay, I'm not going to quit. Our conversations have helped me get a good grasp on leading my church as a solo pastor, but now what? How do I move forward?"

BILL'S QUESTION is a good one, and the story of Nehemiah provides good wisdom. Let's start there.

1. Leading as a solo pastor starts with you.

Moving a church forward always begins with the person God has called and placed in a position of leadership. The book of Nehemiah begins, "The words of Nehemiah" (1:1). Nehemiah did not end up leading the people in Jerusalem by accident. As the cupbearer to King Artaxerxes, he had the knowledge, skills, and connections (network) to accomplish God's calling. He was uniquely prepared to do what God desired for him to do.

The same is true for you. If God has called you to serve as the solo pastor of your church, he has gifted and prepared you to succeed. Each person is unique, with differing backgrounds, training, experiences, struggles, passions, and gifts. So start by canceling any reservations you might have for a guilt trip and accept the reality that God has prepared you to lead the church you are currently serving.

2. Embrace your passions.

God stirred up a passionate concern in Nehemiah's mind and heart for the Jews in Jerusalem who were "in great distress and reproach" (1:3). His concern arose directly from his family, for it was one of his brothers, Hanani, along with some others, who communicated the situation in Jerusalem. Nehemiah most likely had family members in Jerusalem, which heightened his concern and compassion.

God has designed you in such a manner that you have certain concerns that pull you along in ministry. Perhaps you grew up in a broken family and now have a desire to build healthy families through the teaching of God's Word. Or maybe you saw the ravages of alcohol abuse in your uncle's life, and so now you care much about serving broken people, particularly those caught in addiction. Each of us has a unique background that points us in a certain direction. God wants to use what you're passionate about in your church. Get in touch with what God has done in your own life, identify your passions, then see how they align with your church. This may be the vision God wants for your ministry.

3. Beseech God in prayer.

The concerns that grasped Nehemiah's life drove him to prayer and fasting. "I sat down and wept and mourned for days," Nehemiah related, "and I was fasting and praying before the God of

> *When we know, understand, and live the truth, it becomes possible to remain faithful and effective for the long haul.*
>
> —*Brad Powell*

heaven" (1:4). His prayer wasn't a short call to heaven; rather, it lasted for four months, from Chislev to Nisan (v. 1; 2:1). During those months he reflected on God's character, covenant, and commands (1:5); confessed the sins of his people (vv. 6–7); identified personally with the people (vv. 6–7); and asked God to redeem the people's fortunes (vv. 8–10) and for his own success (v. 11). His prayer for success came right before he met personally with the king to ask for assistance. He relates his prayer this way: "O Lord, I beseech You, may Your ear be attentive to the prayer of Your servant and the prayer of Your servants who delight to revere Your name, and make Your servant successful today and grant him compassion before this man" (v. 11).

Your success as a solo pastor is directly tied to the vitality of your prayer life as well as that of the leaders in your church. Moving a church forward is empowered through the prayers of God's people. Through prayer, passion is turned into vision and strategy. Prayer changes hearts, minds, and viewpoints while opening doors of opportunity.

4. Face barriers and powerful people.

Right from the beginning, Nehemiah faced a challenge: King Artaxerxes, the most powerful ruler of that time, had previously decreed that the work of rebuilding Jerusalem had to stop until he issued a new decree to allow work on the city to resume (Ezra 4:17–23). Nehemiah was well aware of this challenge, and he used that insight in knowing how best to proceed and prosper in his request to return to Jerusalem.

A wise solo pastor takes the time to know the church's history, the people, and the issues. This may take some time but can be accomplished in about one year of intense listening and investigation. Discovering the DNA of the church and its leaders provides a solid foundation to build future ministry. Learning about the ups and downs, successes and failures, delights and low lights of the people reveals obstacles—major issues—to future movement.

5. *Design a strategy.*

Nehemiah had served as the cupbearer to Artaxerxes for a number of years (1:11). Cupbearers selected and served the wine and tasted it to protect the king from poisoning. They also served as companions to the king and as keepers of the signet ring, administrated the accounts, and wielded considerable influence. Through his work, Nehemiah knew he had to design an effective strategy to obtain permission to fulfill his vision of rebuilding the wall of Jerusalem. Timing and approach were crucial to gaining approval for his dream, and Nehemiah wisely thought through both as he developed his strategy.

Legend suggests that Artaxerxes showed particular generosity at the first feast of the new year by fulfilling a request made to him at this time. This was called the "Law of the Feast." Aware of this custom, Nehemiah approached the king at the new year's feast, strategically letting the king see his obvious sorrow. By doing so, Nehemiah aroused the king's interest and concern, which prompted a crucial conversation. Upon seeing Nehemiah's sadness, the king said, "Why is your face sad though you are not sick? This is nothing but sadness of heart" (2:2). Nehemiah answered in a manner to elicit the king's sympathy. Respect for ancestral tombs was universal in the ancient Near East, especially among nobility and royalty. With this knowledge, Nehemiah answered the king's question by emphasizing the desolation of his ancestors' tombs: "Why should my face not be sad when the city, the place of my fathers' tombs, lies desolate and its gates have been consumed by

174

fire?" (v. 3). Nehemiah strategically did not mention rebuilding the wall of Jerusalem at this time.

When asked how to renew a church, one leader said, "You have to talk to the right person, at the right time, in the right way, with the right words." Nehemiah followed this admonition well, and so must solo pastors. When designing a strategy, determine the right people, right time, right way, and right words. This comes from knowing the church and its people. The better you plan with these four aspects in mind, the greater the potential for success.

6. *Organize a plan.*

It's evident that Nehemiah had thought out a detailed plan regarding his route to get to Jerusalem, the necessary legal documents, the resources required to do the work, and the time it would take to finish the project. When Artaxerxes asked, "What would you request?" (2:4), Nehemiah was prepared to answer in detail. "Send me to Judah, to the city of my fathers' tombs, that I may rebuild it" (v. 5). The king replied, "How long will your journey be, and when will you return?" (v. 6), to which Nehemiah had definite answers. He also asked for and received the necessary legal documents (v. 7) and vouchers for needed supplies (v. 8).

As a solo pastor, you should think through both strategy and plan. Strategy concerns time and approach, while a plan includes projections of time, resources, legal documents, and organizational structure. Whatever ideas you bring to a church, you must anticipate what questions will be raised and have ready answers, often detailed answers. Pastors who approach church leaders and the congregation with visionary ideas but without a plan that has been carefully thought through will meet resistance. Time spent detailing a plan for a projected vision pays dividends later on, as it encourages the church to move forward.

7. *Investigate your context.*

After a short time in Jerusalem, Nehemiah took the time to study his context: the city, the people, and their needs. He took just a few people along while he checked out the water supply (wells), the gates, the wall, and the various valleys and routes of travel. Although he had a vision of what he hoped to accomplish, he didn't tell the people about it but studied the situation (2:11–16).

There are always at least three perspectives: the solo pastor's, the congregation's, and the community's. Before communicating a vision, you must study all three perspectives to understand how best to frame a vision and a plan for the future.

8. Gain the ownership of the people.

Once Nehemiah had a good understanding of the entire situation, he communicated the needs to the people and challenged them to get involved in rebuilding the walls. At this point, he shared his own story, which led the people to agree to his vision and plan (2:17–18).

At first, it's good for a solo pastor to do some private investigation, but eventually the people have to be brought along so they see the need and opportunity. Pastors often fail at the point of creating a sense of urgency or an understanding of the church's need for a fresh direction. Before presenting your vision to the leaders and full congregation, spend as much time as needed to help others see and believe in the need for a fresh direction. It also helps if you can tie your own passionate story to the new direction.

9. Prepare for resistance.

After Nehemiah arrived in Jerusalem, he found that the leaders were not happy. "When Sanballat the Horonite and Tobiah the Ammonite official heard about it, it was very displeasing to them that someone had come to seek the welfare of the sons of Israel" (2:10). Sanballat was governor of Samaria, and Tobiah was likely a junior colleague of his who was the overseer of Jerusalem. Thus, Nehemiah's coming may have displaced him.

New leadership, fresh ideas, and a new direction always result in some level of opposition. A person once quipped, "If you wish to see the stars, darkness is necessary." The darkness of resistance makes the vision more beautiful. People who lose power and control in a church often fight back, like Tobiah, especially if they have been removed from a cherished role or position. Resistance follows a predictable pattern. It begins with asking critical questions (2:19), moves to anger and attempting to draw others into the argument (4:1), spirals into conspiracy (vv. 7–8), and escalates to physical threats (6:1–2).

Nehemiah's approach to managing resistance is instructive. When people asked questions, he graciously answered (2:20); when they got angry, he prayed (4:4–5); when they conspired against him, he prayed and set up a guard (v. 9); when they threatened him physically, he avoided them (6:3); and, finally, he confronted Tobiah and removed him (13:4–8). Hopefully you won't face such escalation in resistance, but if you do, you might want to follow a similar process: gracious answers, prayer, setting up protections, avoidance, and confrontation when necessary.

10. Remember that the ministry is God's.

Nehemiah took action, but it's clear that he always recognized God was working in and through him to accomplish the rebuilding of the walls. This is seen in the fact that Nehemiah engaged with God through prayer (1:4–11; 2:4; 4:9), was open to God's leading (7:5), encouraged the teaching of the law (8:2–9), restored the observance of proper feasts (v. 13), and called the people to confess their sin (9:3) and worship God (v. 5). Likewise, God is more concerned about your church than you are. Why? Because it's *his* ministry, and he desires it to succeed. God is everywhere seizing the initiative for saving souls, redeeming conflict, healing hurts, restoring broken lives, and, yes, growing his church (Matt. 16:18). This is usually expressed as God's prevenience, which is the conviction that he is always at work, diligently, redemptively, and strategically leading his church. He was at your church before you were, thus he gets the first, middle, and last words.

As a solo pastor, you must look and watch, asking, "What has and is God doing here? Where are the traces of his grace? What has God set in motion already? Where is the story of God's love expressed among these people? What is God already doing, and how can I get on board?" Your job is not so much to come up with a vision as to discover what God is doing and live appropriately with it. Vision is essentially the incarnation of God's will in a particular church, and he often is doing something fresh and new. If you can grasp God's vision, you'll receive his provision.

As you lean in to what God is doing, understand there are two types of success: evident and latent. Evident success is what you can see happening. More people show up at worship, more people are baptized, more people volunteer. This is the visible, tangible fruit of your labor. All pastors rejoice when they see evident success. Another type of success is difficult to see but is there: latent success. Latent means "capable of becoming." It is the movement within people's minds, hearts, and souls. It is the change of attitudes, viewpoints, and perspectives within people's minds. It is the growth in maturity not yet evident. It is active but not yet visible. Leadership maturity means, in part, that you continue faithfully teaching, training, encouraging, discussing, and motivating the congregation onward without visible gratification. It is a reflection of Paul's words to the Corinthians: "Therefore, my beloved brethren, be steadfast, immovable, always abounding in the work of the Lord, knowing that your toil is not in vain in the Lord" (1 Cor. 15:58).

11. Anchor your self-worth in Christ Jesus.
People in our churches live life like they are sitting on a three-legged stool. One leg is their professional life, one is their spiritual life, and the other is their family life. The advantage of a three-legged stool is that it keeps one in balance. For solo pastors, these three legs blur together into one leg, which is inherently unstable. It's difficult for a pastor to separate vocation from family from

personal spirituality, and that's the challenge. The complexity, demands, and loneliness of ministry creep into all areas of one's life. The pastor's self-worth is always under stress from one direction or another, which affects every aspect of life.

Nehemiah was ridiculed and threatened (4:1–3). It's unlikely he could have endured without faith in God's calling in his life and ministry. The same is true for solo pastors. Remaining healthy in ministry as a solo pastor boils down to this: you are in Christ! Ephesians is instructive at this point. Solo pastors (others too) are blessed with every spiritual blessing in Christ (1:3), are predestined to adoption as sons through Christ (vv. 4–6), are redeemed through his blood (v. 7), have obtained an inheritance in him (v. 11), have hope in Christ (v. 12), and are sealed in him by the Holy Spirit (v. 13). "God causes all things to work together for good to those who love God, and to those who are called according to His purpose" (Rom. 8:28). And his purpose is defined in the following verse: for us "to become conformed to the image of His Son" (v. 29). God is interested in you becoming conformed to the image of Christ. God is growing you through success and failure, victory and defeat, criticism and applause. Since you've trusted him with your salvation, you can trust him with your ministry. As you anchor your self-worth and confidence in Christ Jesus, you'll become a catalyst for releasing ministry, coaching volunteers, steering the church toward the future, confronting church bullies, casting vision, and working through resistance.

12. Seize the day; cease your work.

One tension all solo pastors experience is balancing abiding and abounding. Paul encouraged the Corinthians to abound in the work of the Lord (1 Cor. 15:58). Jesus never criticized his disciples for their ambition. Most of the twelve disciples were men of action (fishermen, businessmen, and zealots). Jesus may have selected them because he knew they were self-starters and would actively take the gospel to the ends of the known world.

In tension with abounding is Jesus's call to "abide in Me, and I in you. As the branch cannot bear fruit of itself unless it abides in the vine, so neither can you unless you abide in Me" (John 15:4). Christ's words point to the importance of spiritual connection, and he demonstrated it when he abounded in ministry to the multitudes and then withdrew into the wilderness to abide in solitude with the Father. It's a tension that confronts every pastor or ministry leader. You must take action when it's needed, but you must also rest when it's needed. Find a way to balance activity and quietness, performance and simple presence, abounding and abiding.

THERE ARE DIFFERENT TYPES of pilots, each with different training and responsibilities. Recreational pilots fly primarily for fun and are limited to going only about fifty miles from an airport. Sports pilots are also limited to when, how far, and how high they can fly. They too fly aircraft for their own enjoyment. Private pilots are the most common type. With added certification, they are able to fly at night, carry more passengers, and fly higher than the first two types. Transport pilots fly commercial planes and hold one of the most advanced certificates. Commercial pilots fly sophisticated aircraft with retractable landing gear and must have more precision and knowledge for professional flight operations. The last type of pilot is a flight instructor. They pass on their knowledge and experience to others, whether they be new pilots, veterans, or those just aspiring to fly.

Being a solo pastor is thrilling, but, as with pilots, a solo pastor is only one of many types of pastors. It is, however, the most common type of pastor. It takes a great deal of skill to successfully lead a church as a solo pastor, and this book has covered some of the basics of doing so fruitfully.

Now it's time to put on your flight helmet, position your goggles, strap on your seat belt, and taxi to the runway. It's time to take off and solo on your own. You can do it!

— THREE QUESTIONS

1. Do you identify with any part of Jim and Bill's conversation? If so, which parts and why do you resonate with them?
2. Have you ever thought about quitting ministry? What caused you to feel that way? What kept you going in ministry?
3. What part of Nehemiah's story did you find most helpful? Why?

— TWO IDEAS

1. After you've finished reading *The Solo Pastor*, find a time to get away from the church building and go to a place where you can have a few hours to think and pray with no interruptions. Take a few minutes to glance back through the pages of *The Solo Pastor*. Is there a chapter that stands out in your mind as having special significance for you? Reread that chapter, or perhaps look back over the markings or underlines you made throughout the book. Consider what meaning they had or have to you and your ministry.
2. After you've reflected on your reading of *The Solo Pastor*, list a minimum of three action steps you will take in the next six months. Now—take off! Get going and do them. You'll be glad you did, and so will your church.

Notes

Take Lessons First

1. "Religious Congregations in 21st Century America," National Congregations Study, 2015, https://sites.duke.edu/ncsweb/files/2019/02/NCSIII_report_final.pdf, 14.

2. I sent an email to denominational leaders between February 13, 2021, and May 21, 2021, asking for statistics on the number of churches with solo pastors—that is, those serving alone without any other pastoral staff. The lowest figure was 43 percent and the highest was 95 percent, for an average of 77 percent. All were national church bodies. A total of 53,133 congregations were represented.

Chapter 5 Stop Playing Fetch

1. "Profile of Today's Pastors: Transitions," *Your Church* 41, no. 3 (May/June 1995): 56.

2. Thom S. Rainer, "Six Reasons Pastoral Tenure May Be Increasing," Thom Rainer.com (blog), March 15, 2017, https://archive.thomrainer.com/2017/03/six-reasons-pastoral-tenure-may-be-increasing/; J. D. Hall, "Why God Has (Likely) Called You to Be a Long-Term Pastor," Pulpit & Pen, September 19, 2015, https://pulpitandpen.org/2015/09/19/why-god-has-likely-called-you-to-be-a-long-term-pastor/.

Chapter 7 Communicate Well

1. Paul Jankowski, "5 Ways to Break Through the Noise," *Forbes*, August 24, 2016, https://www.forbes.com/sites/pauljankowski/2016/08/24/5-ways-to-break-through-the-noise/?sh=7f9c6b851d2f.

Chapter 8 Establish Direction

1. For help on how to align resources with goals, see "The Planning Gap," chapter 14 in Gary L. McIntosh, *Here Today, There Tomorrow* (Indianapolis: Wesleyan Publishing House, 2010), 183–92.

Chapter 11 Conquer Fear

1. Kirk B. Jones, "Busyness," *Leadership Journal* (Spring 2001): 42.
2. Gary L. McIntosh, "A Biblical Standard of Success," *Church Growth: America* (July–August 1981): 4–7, 13.
3. Josh Powell, "Back to the Basics," *Outreach* (January/February 2015): 126.
4. Jones, "Busyness," 43.
5. The BREW acronym is from Jones, "Busyness," 43.

Chapter 12 Redeem Stress

1. "38% of U.S. Pastors Have Thought about Quitting Full-Time Ministry in the Past Year," Barna Research, November 16, 2021, https://www.barna.com/research/pastors-well-being/; Scott McConnell, "Are More Pastors Quitting Today?," Lifeway Research, May 13, 2021, https://research.lifeway.com/2021/05/13/are-more-pastors-quitting-today/.
2. Lance Witt, "70% of Pastors Don't Have One," Sermon Central, February 2, 2021, https://www.sermoncentral.com/pastors-preaching-articles/lance-witt-70-of-pastors-don-t-have-one-2480.
3. Amy Frykholm, "Fit for Ministry: Addressing the Crisis in Clergy Health," *Christian Century*, October 22, 2012, https://www.christiancentury.org/article/2012-10/fit-ministry.
4. Cindi May, "A Learning Secret: Don't Take Notes on a Laptop," *Scientific American*, June 3, 2014, https://www.scientificamerican.com/article/a-learning-secret-don-t-take-notes-with-a-laptop/.

Take Flight

1. Adapted from Gordon MacDonald, "The Quiet Strength of a Peaceful Leader," *Leadership Journal* (Spring 2014): 87–88.

About the Author

Gary L. McIntosh serves as distinguished affiliate professor of Christian ministry and leadership at Talbot School of Theology, Biola University, where he has taught courses in the field of pastoral theology for thirty-seven years. He is a professor in the Talbot Doctor of Ministry program, where he leads the Growing and Multiplying Churches cohort and serves as a dissertation mentor.

Dr. McIntosh has forty years of experience consulting for nonprofit organizations, coaching leaders, and giving seminar presentations. He has analyzed numerous churches representing more than ninety denominations throughout the United States, Canada, Australia, and several countries in Southeast Asia. His articles have appeared in numerous publications. He is editor of the *Growth Points* leadership newsletter and has written or co-authored twenty-seven books, including *Overcoming the Dark Side of Leadership* (1998), *One Size Doesn't Fit All* (1999), *Staff Your Church for Growth* (2000), *Biblical Church Growth* (2003), *Beyond the First Visit* (2006), *Taking Your Church to the Next Level* (2009), *There's Hope for Your Church* (2012), *Being the Church in a Multi-Ethnic Community* (2012), *What Every Pastor Should Know* (2013), *Donald A. McGavran: A Biography of the*

Twentieth Century's Premier Missiologist (2015), *Growing God's Church* (2016), *Building the Body* (2017), and *The Ten Key Roles of a Pastor* (2021).

Dr. McIntosh has received several awards, including the Talbot School of Theology Dean's Award, Biola University's Robert B. Fisher Faculty Excellence Award, Colorado Christian University's Distinguished Alumni Award, Fuller Theological Seminary's Donald McGavran Award, the McGavran Award from the American Society for Church Growth, the Lifetime Achievement Award from Church Leader Insights, and the Win Arn Lifetime Achievement Award from the Great Commission Research Network.

Gary and his wife, Carol, reside in Temecula, California. They have two grown sons and seven grandchildren.

Dr. McIntosh is available for speaking or consulting. For information, please contact Dr. McIntosh at the Church Growth Network, PO Box 892589, Temecula, CA 92589-2589, (951) 506-3086.

Connect with
GARY

ChurchGrowthNetwork.com

 drgmcintosh   garymcintosh1

Learn to Lead Your Church More Effectively

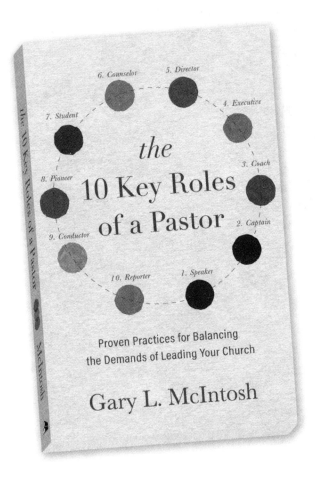

Pastors can feel overwhelmed too. Whether you're just starting out in ministry or you've been at it for a while, this practical resource will help you live and lead more fruitfully in your calling.

BakerBooks
a division of Baker Publishing Group
www.BakerBooks.com

Available wherever books and ebooks are sold.

REACHING A CHANGING WORLD WITH THE UNCHANGING GOSPEL

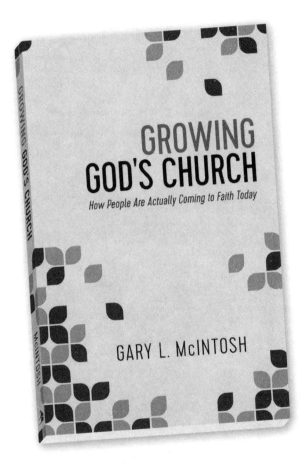

Based on ten years of comprehensive research, *Growing God's Church* unveils how people are actually coming to faith in the twenty-first century.

BakerBooks
a division of Baker Publishing Group
www.BakerBooks.com

Available wherever books and ebooks are sold.

THE ANSWERS YOU NEED TO PLAN, RUN, OR GROW YOUR CHURCH

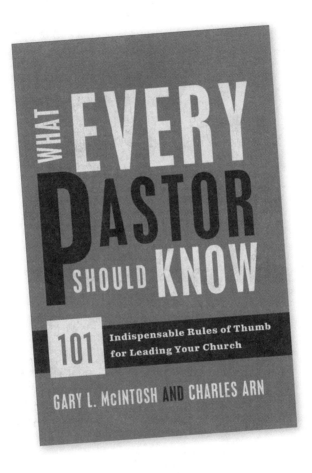

101 valuable rules and time-tested wisdom to help answer real-life ministry questions. From advertising to facilities to visitation, this indispensable book offers the practical help you need, just when you need it most.

BakerBooks
a division of Baker Publishing Group
www.BakerBooks.com

Available wherever books and ebooks are sold.

Connect with

BakerBooks
Relevant. Intelligent. Engaging.

Sign up for announcements about
new and upcoming titles at

BakerBooks.com/SignUp

@ReadBakerBooks